Praise for *Leading Collective Efficacy: Powerful Stories of Achievement and Equity*

"If you want your building to become a warm and welcoming place with a caring staff where all children become lifelong learners, you want to read this book! Collective efficacy will positively impact and transform your school. It will help close your achievement gap and make your children feel safe and loved."

—Concetta Lupo
Principal, Blue Bell Elementary School

"Dr. Arzonetti Hite and Dr. Donohoo's *Leading Collective Efficacy: Powerful Stories of Achievement and Equity* provides a pragmatic approach to creating a framework as schools work to foster collective teacher efficacy. The vignettes are relatable and the reflective questions posed throughout help guide leaders as they work to initiate systemic change. If you're looking to provide structures that support teachers to engage in collaborative cycles of inquiry, this book is a great place to start. I look forward to sharing this book with my colleagues as we work to move 'from a focus on individual accountability to collective impact.'"

—Kelly Harmon
Director of Curriculum & Instruction,
Monmouth County Vocational School District

"Rarely do you find a book that readily addresses the needs of so many departments across education. *Leading Collective Efficacy: Powerful Stories of Achievement and Equity* should be within arm's reach of every school teacher, coach, teaching union, principal, inspector, and district administrator. The authors unpack the theory and underpinnings of collective teacher efficacy and then bring them to life with case studies demonstrating mastery experiences and vicarious experiences. The result is that readers feel emboldened to bring this to bear on their own context, whether at national or district level or within their own school.

The generosity of the educators who have honestly shared their journeys in this book is commendable and is a reflection of the standing of, and trust in, Arzonetti Hite and Donohoo in education leadership."

—Caroline Martin

Chief Psychologist, City of Dublin Education and Training Board

"In this book, Drs. Arzonetti Hite and Donohoo provide specific protocols and designs to apply collective efficacy in a school or district setting. By using case studies and exemplars, they outline specific ways in which collective efficacy has been directly implemented across different educational settings, thereby bringing new understandings of ways it might be realized in other places."

—Carl Atkinson

Retired Assistant Superintendent

"This book is a great read! As a leader and researcher, I appreciate how this book is backed by validated research and develops upon each enabling condition of collective efficacy through the experiences of educators!"

—Dana Jamison

Elementary Principal, Muscoy Elementary School

Leading Collective Efficacy

Leading Collective Efficacy

Powerful Stories of Achievement and Equity

Stefani Arzonetti Hite
and Jenni Donohoo

FOR INFORMATION

Corwin
A SAGE Company
2455 Teller Road
Thousand Oaks, California 91320
(800) 233-9936
www.corwin.com

SAGE Publications Ltd.
1 Oliver's Yard
55 City Road
London EC1Y 1SP
United Kingdom

SAGE Publications India Pvt. Ltd.
B 1/I 1 Mohan Cooperative Industrial Area
Mathura Road, New Delhi 110 044
India

SAGE Publications Asia-Pacific Pte. Ltd.
18 Cross Street #10-10/11/12
China Square Central
Singapore 048423

Printed in the United States of America

Library of Congress Cataloging-in-Publication Data

Names: Hite, Stefani Arzonetti, author. | Donohoo, Jenni, author.

Title: Leading collective efficacy : powerful stories of achievement and equity / Stefani Arzonetti Hite and Jenni Donohoo.

Description: Thousand Oaks, California : Corwin Press, Inc, 2021. | Includes bibliographical references.

Identifiers: LCCN 2020030637 | ISBN 9781071801802 (paperback) | ISBN 9781071801796 (epub) | ISBN 9781071801789 (epub) | ISBN 9781071801772 (ebook)

Subjects: LCSH: Professional learning communities—United States. | Professional learning communities—Canada. | Educational leadership—United States. | Educational leadership—Canada. | Teacher-administrator relationships—United States. | Teacher-administrator relationships—Canada. | Academic achievement—United States. | Academic achievement—Canada.

Classification: LCC LB1731 .H534 2021 | DDC 370.71/1—dc23

LC record available at https://lccn.loc.gov/2020030637

This book is printed on acid-free paper.

Program Director and Publisher: Dan Alpert
Senior Content Development Editor: Lucas Schleicher
Associate Content Development Editor: Mia Rodriguez
Production Editor: Tori Mirsadjadi
Copy Editor: Terri Lee Paulsen
Typesetter: Hurix Digital
Proofreader: Liann Lech
Indexer: Integra
Cover Designer: Lysa Becker
Marketing Manager: Lisa Lysne

20 21 22 23 24 10 9 8 7 6 5 4 3 2 1

Contents

Chapter 3: Empowered Teachers   38

Chapter 4: Cohesive Teacher Knowledge   55

List of Figures and Tables

Acknowledgments

We'd like to thank our editor, Dan Alpert, who first shone a light on the equity lens that emerged in the stories of achievement. We'd also like to thank Tim O'Leary and John Hattie, who helped to validate the enabling conditions for the collective teacher efficacy scale.

Of course, the power of collective efficacy relies on the people we have worked with who were willing to share their stories: Jill Geocaris, Ken Wallace, Denise Cleary, Derek Kondratowicz, Reina Irizarry-Clark, Lisa Pryor, Mike Pekosz, D'Les Gonzales Herron, and Garth Larson. We'd also like to acknowledge the hard work and passion of the teachers in the schools and districts featured throughout this book.

Finally, we would also like to acknowledge our families for their unwavering support and for sacrificing time with us as we worked on this project.

Preface

The Importance of Collective Teacher Efficacy

The concept of collective efficacy has become increasingly important in educational circles over the past decade. The main reason is that collective teacher efficacy has remained at the top of Hattie's (2019) list of factors that influence student achievement. Collective teacher efficacy refers to a staff's shared belief that through their collective action they can positively influence student outcomes, including those of students who are disengaged and/or disadvantaged. There is a strong positive relationship between collective teacher efficacy and student achievement. An abundance of research demonstrates that schools that have a firmly established sense of collective efficacy (and are otherwise similar) have higher student achievement. This is because when collective efficacy is present, it results in greater persistence, increased motivation, and sustained effort required to implement evidence-based practices that help to support student learning (Donohoo & Katz, 2020). Goddard, Skrla, and Salloum (2017) demonstrated that collective teacher efficacy not only fosters high overall achievement but it also results in reduction of achievement gaps. Clearly, it's important for district leaders, school leaders, informal leaders, and classroom educators to understand what collective teacher efficacy is and why it is important in relation to improving student outcomes and confronting and addressing inequity.

Over the past few years we have seen numerous social media posts in which collective efficacy is the topic. Many depict teams engaged in trust- and community-building activities and challenges. For example, a recent post on Twitter showed teachers standing next to a free-standing structure made completely of paper straws and the

> Collective teacher efficacy refers to a staff's shared belief that through their collective action they can positively influence student outcomes, including those of students who are disengaged and/or disadvantaged.

Readers will gain a better understanding of ways to capitalize on the reciprocal relationship between increased student achievement and collective teacher efficacy in schools by learning about how others have accomplished it.

"Narratives that cause us to pay attention and also involve us emotionally are the stories that motivate us to action" (Zak, 2015).

The real-life examples shared throughout demonstrate how through perseverant effort districts, schools, and teams were able to overcome the disadvantages associated with low income, lack of English-language proficiency, and race and/or ethnicity.

caption read, "Which team can build the tallest straw structure? What a great way to build #collectiveefficacy." Another showed teachers in a gymnasium enthusiastically engaged in a game of human Hungry, Hungry Hippos with the caption, "Great efficacy building activity." In both examples, teachers appeared to be happy and connected to each other. We agree that laughter, connection, trust, and community building are incredibly essential in the workplace. However, there is a big difference between building community and developing teachers' sense of collective efficacy. Hattie (personal communication) noted that collective efficacy is more complicated than just making teachers feel good about themselves and their colleagues.

Educators are beginning to recognize the importance of fostering collective teacher efficacy. The question is how you go about doing so. Educators are asking, *What does collective efficacy really look like? How does it improve student achievement and decrease achievement gaps? How can we accomplish it in our school?* This book contains stories of what collective efficacy looks like in districts, in schools, and among teams who have actualized it in practice. Readers will gain a better understanding of ways to capitalize on the reciprocal relationship between increased student achievement and collective teacher efficacy in schools by learning about how others have accomplished it. We chose to share case studies because we recognize both the power of stories and the importance of providing exemplars. Powerful stories help us achieve large-scale goals. They do this by captivating our attention, compelling us to take action, and influencing our behavior so that we make permanent changes that have a lasting impact (Hall, 2019).

The stories highlighted in this book support what research has demonstrated about the strong and positive relationship between collective teacher efficacy and improved student achievement. They also highlight how collective efficacy plays a critical role in addressing educational inequities by demonstrating the role of collective teacher efficacy in closing achievement gaps. The real-life examples shared throughout demonstrate how, through perseverant effort, districts, schools, and teams were able to overcome the disadvantages associated with low income, lack of English-language proficiency, and race and/or ethnicity. Confronting inequity is one of the greatest challenges facing schools today, and it requires that educators build the adaptive capacity to meet that challenge.

As Goddard et al. (2017) demonstrated, "The stronger a school's sense of collective efficacy, the higher the overall levels of mathematics achievement *and* the lower the disadvantage for Black students. One standard deviation increase in collective efficacy was associated with a 50% reduction in the academic disadvantage experienced by Black students" (p. 10). "In addition, Latino students did not score significantly differently than White students after accounting for their prior achievement, ethnicity, gender, and status with regard to ESL, special education, and free or reduced-price lunch programs" (p. 11).

VIGNETTE 0.1

Closing the Achievement Gap

When Blake Johnson (pseudonym) arrived as the principal at Tallamore High School, he had his work cut out for him. The school had a negative reputation and was located in a low-socioeconomic area of a mid-sized New England city. Every student in the school qualified for free and reduced-price lunch. Students were underperforming on standardized state tests and the graduation rate was only 63 percent. By attending to the enabling conditions for collective efficacy, Blake and the teachers at Tallamore High School were able to make significant improvement. Five years later, 81.3 percent of Black students at Tallamore High School scored proficient or above on the state academic performance test, when only 59.7 percent of Black students in the state achieved proficiency. Furthermore, the achievement gap between Black students and white

Evans (2009) noted that "inevitably, race, class, and the school's social environment affect the academic content and skills teachers choose to teach and their beliefs about students' ability to learn, as well as beliefs about their own ability to improve student performance" (p. 66). Evans refers to this as the "proverbial catch-22." Schools with low-performing, poor, and/or minority students are faced with the challenge of closing achievement gaps, while teachers and leaders in these schools doubt their collective ability to improve the performance of low-achieving students.

students was eliminated. That year, Tallamore High School was nationally recognized for its achievement.

Blake described what was going on in the school when he arrived as "curricular chaos." He said "a curriculum didn't exist or teachers were using a program and mistaking it as curriculum. Not one teacher was on the same page because we didn't even have a page." Most of the teachers' unspoken expectations of Mr. Johnson that first year were "you leave us alone and we'll leave you alone." A culture of resistance to examining data and lack of evidence-based decision-making was prevalent. In addition, Blake often overheard sweeping generalizations from some of the staff about the students at the school. These included references about what "these kids" were not capable of accomplishing. Furthermore, Blake noted there was an absence of instructional leadership, accountability, and efficacy. Many on staff believed that "whatever they did to try to positively influence student achievement, it wasn't going to make a difference."

Blake's leadership philosophy centered around three important ideas: work hard, be nice, and get better. He focused collaboration and instructional improvement efforts on three critical questions: *What* are we teaching? *How* are we teaching? And *who* are we teaching? Blake indicated that feelings of discomfort, unhappiness, and disequilibrium are natural "fallouts from creating change in schools." He knew, however, that by being supportive to teachers and standing by the core belief of keeping what's best for students front and center, he could convince the faculty that they had the ability to make an educational difference to the students at Tallamore High School regardless of students' home and community circumstances.

Blake began by building time into the master schedule for each core academic area to create common formative assessments and prioritize standards so that every teacher would be "crystal clear about what we wanted our students to know and be able to do." He identified teacher leaders as he recognized that he would need "someone with the expertise and ability to facilitate that kind of learning." He got teachers to buy in to goals by ensuring the goals and outcome measures were meaningful to teachers and linked to their content areas. He also provided opportunities for teachers to learn more about each other's practices through coaching, micro-teaching, and peer observation.

Blake described a moment when he knew the narrative was shifting from what wasn't possible (meeting students' diverse needs) to what was possible (getting better). Teachers had the opportunity every year to attend summer institutes. During these institutes it was typically experienced teachers who attended to create lessons, teach them in front of their peers while being videotaped, and then receive feedback. During the second summer, when the summer institute filled up, Blake noted a tipping point when teachers who were struggling began attending. Blake said "they felt safe enough to come into a vulnerable environment. When you have teachers buying in to getting better as a professional, you know something is starting to take root."

Leading Collective Teacher Efficacy

In this book, we outline a model for leading collective teacher efficacy in schools (Figure 0.1), which includes five enabling conditions that have been validated, through research (Donohoo, O'Leary, & Hattie, 2020), as school characteristics associated with collective teacher efficacy. These include gaining consensus on goals, empowering teachers, building cohesive teacher knowledge, and embedding reflective practices, which are all accomplished through supportive leadership. While enabling conditions do not *cause* things to happen, they increase the likelihood that things will turn out as intended.

Figure 0.1   A Model for Leading Collective Teacher Efficacy

In our model, the outer ring represents supportive leadership. While it is one of the five identified conditions that foster collective efficacy, supportive leaders play a crucial role in strengthening the other four enabling conditions. Bandura's (1998) four sources of efficacy—mastery experiences, vicarious experiences, social persuasion, and affective states (illustrated on the inner ring of the circle)—are activated when teachers are empowered, cohesive teacher knowledge and goal consensus exist, and reflective practices are embedded as part of the normative expectations of teachers' everyday work. We will share more about the sources of efficacy and the enabling conditions in Chapter 1. Each subsequent chapter takes a closer look at one of the enabling conditions through the experiences of educators across North America.

In Blake Johnson's approach, through his supportive leadership, he was attending to the enabling conditions for collective teacher efficacy.

Goal Consensus

Blake indicated that it was too long of a wait to see if progress was being made on standardized assessments, in which the results were released annually, so he helped teachers set intermediary goals around the common assessments *they* created. He also knew that in order for teachers to buy in to goals, the goals needed to be short term and linked to teachers' content areas in relation to the standards.

Empowered Teachers

Recognizing that he couldn't do it all, Blake believed in the importance of growing people and delegating leadership responsibilities. He created leadership positions that provided teacher leaders with decision-making power over important issues related to instructional improvement.

Cohesive Teacher Knowledge

When Blake first arrived at the school, he described it as the "wild, wild West" and the faculty as "independent contractors—everyone was doing their own thing." By keeping the three questions in the forefront (*What* are we teaching? *How* are we teaching? *Who* are we teaching?) and by structuring opportunities for teachers to engage in micro-teaching and peer observation, Blake was building cohesion in regard to a shared understanding of effective pedagogical practices.

Embedded Reflective Practices

Blake provided time and support so that teachers could create common formative assessments and plans for intervention during the school day.

Teacher teams, facilitated by the department head, came to consensus on essential understandings they wanted their students to know and every 3 to 4 weeks administered a common assessment. *The next day*, teachers engaged in moderated marking and determined plans for remediation or enrichment based on the information from the assessments. Blake noted that it was important to provide time for teachers to analyze student work, based on the goals, before moving on to the next unit. That way, teachers were "better able to respond to the data."

Supportive Leadership

Blake indicated that "it's all about relationships—especially when providing feedback to teachers. Teachers have to know that you care about them." Blake used the term *touches* to describe positive connections between two people. "Touches build relationships, and the closer you are, the more likely you are to receive and act upon feedback."

The reciprocal relationship between collective teacher efficacy and improved student results was realized at Tallamore High School. As noted earlier, the achievement gap between Black students and white students was eliminated; 81.3 percent of Black students and 82.1 percent of white students scored proficient or above on the state academic performance test in Blake's fifth year as principal. Blake also noted that disciplinary office referrals declined and that "teachers felt good about what they were accomplishing."

> "School processes that contribute to a cohesive, supportive climate are likely to contribute to each of the four sources of efficacy information, especially the most powerful mastery experiences" (Ross, Hogaboam-Gray, & Gray, 2004, p. 168).

Sources of Collective Teacher Efficacy

By attending to these enabling conditions, Blake tapped into sources of collective teacher efficacy. The interactions that Blake created among teachers influenced how they interpreted progress as evidence of mastery. Teachers' collaborations contributed to their knowledge of each other's effectiveness through the collective identification of indicators of students' progress toward goals. The common formative assessments made it easier for teachers to recognize when they were successful. Ross et al. (2004) noted that "mastery is both an individual and a social construction in which achievements by students are interpreted as evidence of teacher success and failure, thereby contributing to individual and collective teacher efficacy" (p. 166).

Although mastery is the most potent source of efficacy (Bandura, 1986), vicarious experiences are also a powerful efficacy-shaping source. Peer observations and increased collaboration among teachers at Tallamore High School provided opportunities for them to recognize the contributions of the collective to individual success. The environment created was one where help seeking was encouraged, consensus was built around goals, and there were opportunities for authentic decision-making. As a result, teachers gained clarity and common understanding of effective instruction, thereby increasing perceptions of their individual and collective success and expectations for future success.

"As people's sense of efficacy grows stronger, they become more courageous and confident in dealing with difficult circumstances, recasting them in ways that appear more manageable" (Evans, 2009, p. 70).

Bandura's four sources of efficacy information can be provided through school conditions. Among the most powerful are "collaborative school processes that contribute to cohesion and support for teachers" (Ross et al., 2004, p. 168).

Leaders can tap into the sources of collective teacher efficacy by fostering the enabling conditions.

Social persuasion is the third source of efficacy-shaping information identified by Bandura (1986). As teacher teams met with success, those who had experienced successful collaborations in one department would persuade teachers in other departments about the efficacy of the staff. Blake also provided frequent feedback that was explicitly designed to help teachers make the link between their efforts and improved results. As teachers began to attribute success to what it was they were doing as a collective, they reduced their past practice of blaming external factors for their students' performance.

Finally, the fourth source of efficacy is affective states (Bandura, 1986). Affective states can be negative (e.g., fear, anxiety, frustration) or they can be positive (e.g., joy, excitement, accomplishment). Collaborations where peers supported each other helped to diminish the effects of negative emotions and heighten the effects of positive emotions on efficacy. Positive feelings are a direct source of efficacy-shaping information, and teams form their beliefs about what they are collectively capable of accomplishing based on that information. The peer support helped teachers at Tallamore High School build a sense of community that resulted in feelings of optimism and confidence. As one teacher put it, "This has helped me so much I feel better able to support my ELLs [English language learners]."

How to Use This Book

As noted earlier, Chapters 2–6 are organized around the five enabling conditions as a model for leading collective teacher efficacy in schools. Leaders can tap into the sources of collective teacher efficacy by fostering the enabling conditions. As demonstrated at Tallamore High School, the five enabling conditions do not operate in isolation. They are very much interconnected. Readers will learn about how leaders intentionally fostered these conditions within their school environments and how increased student achievement, reduction of achievement gaps, and collective teacher efficacy occurred as a result. While each story focuses on one specific enabling condition, we encourage readers to consider how the conditions complement each other and synergistically interact.

We encourage readers to delve into these powerful stories and consider the following:

1. What prompted the need for change in the school or district?

2. How did the focus on a particular enabling condition allow educators to tap into the sources of efficacy?

3. How did the highlighted enabling condition enhance the other enabling conditions and amplify the impact of teachers' work?

4. What learning protocols and designs allowed educators to structure the work so that it resulted in meaningful collaborative inquiry?

5. What lessons might we learn and apply to our unique learning community?

It is within every leader's scope of influence to support the development of collective efficacy in schools. When we use the term *leaders* throughout this book, we are referring to both formal and informal leaders. Whether you are a system leader, school leader, or teacher leader, the ideas in this book are pertinent if you are interested in developing efficacy. More important than an educator's positional authority is their passion and perseverance in supporting the conditions that foster greater success for all students.

Readers will learn about how leaders intentionally fostered these conditions within their school environments and how increased student achievement, reduction of achievement gaps, and collective teacher efficacy occurred as a result.

It is within every leader's scope of influence to support the development of collective efficacy in schools.

About the Authors

Stefani Arzonetti Hite spent a decade in the marketing industry before switching gears to become a teacher. Shifting gears again, she moved into administration, moved to the UK to run an international school, and then came back to the United States to become a full-time professional learning designer and facilitator. So much shifting of gears—and the result is a pretty deep toolbox.

Stef's world is not complete without a daily dose of coffee, dark chocolate, and the *New York Times* crossword puzzle. Her favorite place to be is home with her husband, daughter, and devilish cats, Merry and Pippin. Her second favorite place to be is visiting some corner of the world because learning often requires roads less traveled.

For the past 10 years, Stef's work has focused on helping teams build collective efficacy so they can learn their way through complex problems. A few years ago, she contacted Jenni and said, "Hey, want to write a book together?" Jenni said yes, and you're holding the result. Enjoy!

Jenni Donohoo is a best-selling author and former classroom teacher who has spent the past 20 years working alongside system and school leaders, coaches, and teachers in leading school improvement. Besides her consulting work and writing, Jenni is a keynote speaker and has presented at many national and international conferences. Jenni's mission is to help shape mastery environments in which everyone in an educational setting shares the belief that individually and collectively they have the capability to impact positive change.

When she is not in schools or on the road, Jenni is at home with her husband, Jim, and their two golden retrievers, Stella and Lucy. They split their time between their home in Amherstburg, Ontario, and their home in New Orleans, Louisiana. Jenni, Jim, Stella, and Lucy enjoy the rich history, music, architecture, restaurants, and doggie parks that the French Quarter has to offer.

When Stef approached Jenni with the idea of writing this book, Jenni knew it was the next important resource needed in the field to advance this work so it was easy to say "yes." We hope you enjoy it.

Educators' Beliefs Matter 1

A Tale of Two School Improvement Teams With Very Different Outlooks

Recently, we were asked by a senior administrator to work with school improvement teams at two of their low-performing high schools. The student demographics at the first school were described by the principal as "high level of poverty, a large number of students in applied level (workplace bound) courses with large gaps in their learning, home-environment issues, large number of students on Individual Education Plans (about 33%), many with mild intellectual disabilities (MID), a transient population, substance abuse, and mental health issues." In fact, 31.6 percent of the students in this high school were receiving special education services, a much higher percentage than the state average of 14.9 percent. The student demographics at the second school were also described by the administrator there as "high poverty and transient population with a large number of students whose first language is not English." Thirty-seven percent of the students came from low-income homes, 20.7 percent were receiving special education services, and the percentage of students whose first language was not English was 47.9 percent—significantly higher than the state average of 23.9 percent.

While both high schools experienced similar challenges and concerns, there was a stark contrast between the beliefs held by the educators in the two schools and these beliefs played out in their practice. During the visit at the first school, a team of teachers presented a plan they had drafted to address the literacy needs of the students in their school and requested feedback. Driving the team's work were the following three essential questions:

1. How can we improve literacy school-wide?

2. How can we increase and maintain an increase in student achievement?

3. How can we assist previously eligible students and special education students to increase their success on standardized tests?

In the plan, the team had listed a number of strategies including "increase whole school awareness of literacy and work together to address the problem" and "build upon students' strengths while also focusing on areas for growth." The plan went on to list actionable steps to take and timelines for doing so, and laid out roles and responsibilities for individuals involved. The conversation around the table was very positive, and teachers talked about things they were learning about and identified a few evidence-based strategies they agreed to try in their own classrooms. They also talked about an upcoming professional development day and began to identify strategies to model for the entire faculty.

Upon entering the meeting room at the second high school, the tone seemed immediately different from what we had experienced at the first school. The body language (crossed arms) and facial expressions (upset/angry) of the teachers in the room seemed to indicate that they were feeling strained and the room was full of tension. They too had considered students' learning needs and identified *basic skill development* as the most pressing of these needs along with student engagement. The team spent a lot of time explaining to us just how challenging the circumstances were at this school, noting that parents were not supportive and that students were coming to school "less and less able to manage themselves." At one point, a teacher said, "I feel ill-equipped to teach many of the students in my class" and went on to say that "everyone in my department is overwhelmed with work." When we tried to nudge the conversation to help the team identify some manageable steps they might take to improve student learning, the principal expressed the "hope to emphasize that this is not more work" and a teacher chimed in by agreeing that "teachers are much more motivated to do something that will make their day easier rather than an add-on; if there is something that can make a teacher's job easier, people will be on board." Finally, the meeting ended with one of the teachers saying, "None of this really matters because there isn't much we can do that is going to make a difference for *these* kids."

Teachers' theories about the relationship between students' race, class, first language, and resulting achievement affect the content and skills teachers choose to teach, their beliefs about students' ability to learn, as well as their beliefs about what they can do to increase student performance (Evans, 2009). In teachers' analysis of their collective capabilities to meet the needs of all students, including those who are disadvantaged, if teachers view this as an unattainable goal, their individual and collective efficacy will be diminished.

> Bandura (2000) noted that "the higher the perceived collective efficacy, the higher the groups' motivational investments in their undertakings, the stronger their staying power in the face of impediments and setbacks, and the greater their performance accomplishments" (p. 78).

Collective Efficacy Beliefs

Collective teacher efficacy is a shared *belief* in a team's combined ability to positively impact student outcomes. It is the "collective self-perception that teachers in a given school make an educational difference to their students over and above the educational impact of their homes and communities" (Tschannen-Moran & Barr, 2004, p. 190). The team at the first high school had a sense of collective efficacy, which was a key factor in motivating *their* productive and collaborative efforts. They responded to difficult challenges with the determination and collective resolve to tackle them head on. The teachers believed that together they could make a difference and they made connections between their joint efforts and the small incremental increases they were realizing in relation to student success.

Collective teacher efficacy is a shared *belief* in a team's combined ability to positively impact student outcomes.

The team at the second school responded to similar issues with resignation and excuses as to why they *couldn't* succeed. They attributed the reasons for their lack of success to external causes. As a result of their lack of collective efficacy, they convinced themselves that their efforts did not matter and therefore, they were not motivated to take action. If the efficacy beliefs of the teachers at this school are not strengthened

Readers will find additional information about the relationship between collective teacher efficacy and student results in Appendix A.

and attributions for success and/or failure are not shifted from external to internal causes, the consequences for the students will remain dire. Issues of inequity will remain unaddressed.

We believe that every educator wants every student to experience academic success. We also believe that educators want to provide students with safe and rich learning environments where every student, regardless of their circumstances at home, English-language proficiency, race, or ethnicity, receives the support they require in order to be successful. Sometimes, however, a diminished sense of efficacy gets in the way of realizing success for all. When educators do not believe they have what it takes to overcome the challenges posed by students' personal or social circumstances, they set lower goals and expend less effort, and often avoidance occurs as a result. Efficacy beliefs influence how individuals and teams "feel, think, motivate themselves, and behave" (Bandura, 1993). When efficacy is lacking, teams are less likely to take

When examining the role of collective efficacy in closing student achievement gaps, Goddard et al. (2017) found that collective efficacy beliefs were important to educational equity and achievement. The researchers found that collective efficacy was associated with a 50 percent reduction in the academic disadvantage experienced by minority students. In the schools with high efficacy, stories were shared in which educators refused to accept excuses for low performance.

risks and lack a willingness to try different approaches. They are less likely to implement evidence-based strategies and less receptive to change. The dilemma, of course, is that as a lack of efficacy results in the avoidance of educator risk-taking and implementation of improvement efforts, student trajectories will remain unchanged. Groups of students who require interventions needed to shift trajectories upward will be the ones to suffer the consequences.

Efficacy Beliefs Drive Receptiveness to Change

As noted earlier, when efficacy *is* well established, teams are more likely to step outside their comfort zones and figure out how to make evidence-based strategies work in their environments, given their unique circumstances and diverse student populations (Donohoo & Katz, 2020). In other words, efficacy beliefs are a precursor to improved student outcomes because efficacy drives educators' receptiveness to change.

Figure 1.1   Receptiveness to Change During Stages of Implementation Matrix

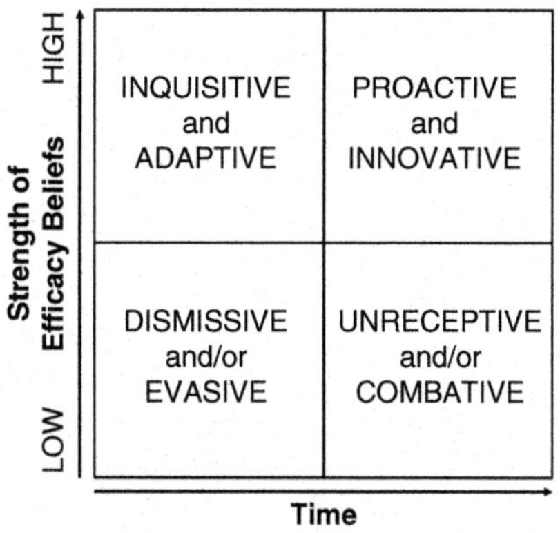

Figure 1.2   Low Efficacy/Beginning Stage of Implementation

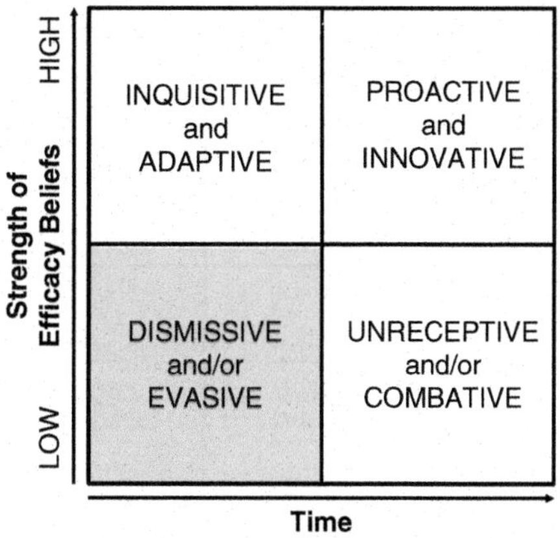

The relationship between efficacy beliefs and receptiveness to change is demonstrated in the matrix shown in Figure 1.1. On the left side, efficacy beliefs range from low to high. Time is represented along the bottom. When change is first introduced in a school, if efficacy beliefs are low (Figure 1.2), teachers are likely to be dismissive and/or evasive, adopting a "this too shall pass" attitude. Rather than taking action, they will wait it out—hoping for a change in administration. These are the teachers who are conveniently absent from professional learning and find excuses to not attend meetings related to the proposed change. If efficacy beliefs are high (Figure 1.3), however, teachers are inquisitive when hearing about proposed changes. Just like the teachers in the first high school, highly efficacious teams pose questions, explore possibilities, and are open to adapting their current practice. They want to learn more.

Figure 1.3   High Efficacy/Beginning Stage of Implementation

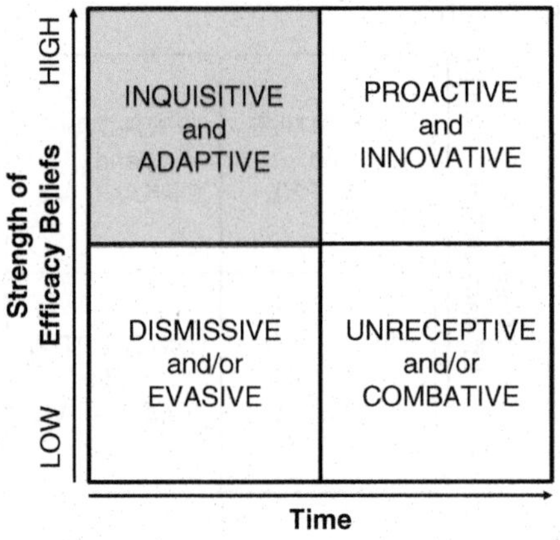

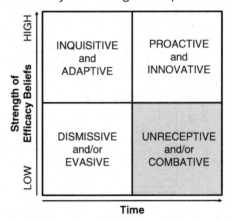

Figure 1.4   Low Efficacy/Later Stage of Implementation

Over time, as expectations for implementation and accountability pressures increase, if efficacy is low (Figure 1.4), teachers will become unreceptive and perhaps even combative. These are the teachers who refuse to try anything new in their classrooms—often because they believe the tasks they are being asked to perform are harder than they actually are. Sometimes, a diminished sense of efficacy manifests itself in a heavy reliance on current practice, and teams protect the status quo rather than express a willingness to inquire into the impact of their practices.

If efficacy is high (Figure 1.5), however, educators are ready to take on change—even before it happens. Teams take control and figure out ways to work things out. Over time, they successfully cope with and support the changes initiated. They become innovative. We do not want to give readers the impression here, however, that our use

Figure 1.5   High Efficacy/Later Stage of Implementation

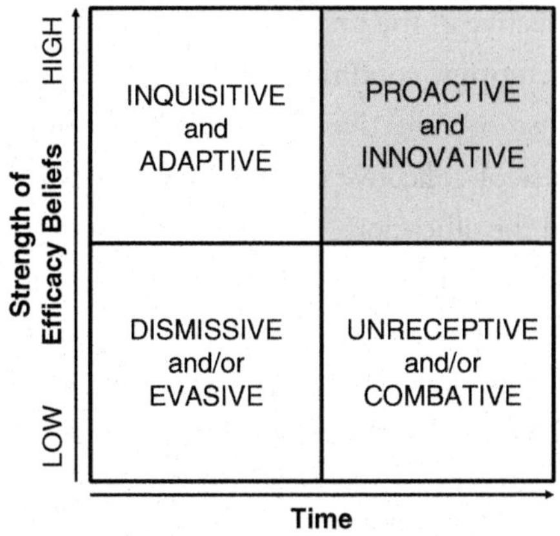

of the term *innovative* suggests that we believe that educators need to invent any new ways of improving schools. That is not the case. We are on fairly solid ground when it comes to the *what* of school improvement. There is a plethora of research about what works in schools that dates back many decades. What we mean by innovative (represented in the top-right quadrant of the matrix) is the deep implementation of evidence-based strategies that are purposefully selected given the unique context of different schools and classrooms. Highly efficacious teams are innovative in the sense that they figure out how to realize the promises of evidence-based, improvement-oriented interventions—regardless of their unique environments and student populations (Donohoo & Katz, 2020). As Tschannen-Moran and Barr (2004) put it, "Teachers in schools with high collective efficacy do not accept low student achievement as an inevitable by-product of low socioeconomic status, lack of ability, or family background. They roll up their sleeves and get the job done" (p. 192).

We developed this matrix to illustrate how receptiveness to change is highly influenced by efficacy beliefs. Without change, there can't be improvement. Without improvement, equity in education will not be achieved. Without a firmly established belief in efficacy, it is unlikely that change resulting in improvement will occur.

Readers probably made connections to their own experiences based on the contrasting shared beliefs held by the teachers at the two high schools in the story

> Robinson (2018) made a deliberate distinction between the terms *change* and *improvement* and noted that with this distinction "there is likely to be more critical and more thoughtful debate before large-scale implementation" (p. 3).

recounted at the beginning of this chapter. Whether readers' current realities are reflective of the first high school or the second, it would be important to determine conditions in schools that lead to the formation of a strong sense of collective efficacy. What was it that contributed to teachers' sense of collective efficacy in the first school? What shared experiences did the efficacious team of high school teachers have in the past? What was in place in the first high school that helped to foster teachers' willingness to collaborate, inquire, adapt, and innovate? It would also be important to consider what undermines efficacy. What caused the teachers in the second school to give up?

The Formation of Efficacy Beliefs

Individual and collective efficacy beliefs are formed based on information processed from past experiences (Bandura, 1986) as well as contextual factors that contribute to teachers' perceptions about their current realities. Efficacy beliefs are future oriented (Bandura, 1986). They are rooted in individuals' and teams' "there and then" experiences (what occurred in the past) and "here and now" experiences (what is happening in the current environment). In the section that follows, sources from past experiences that become efficacy-shaping information will be shared. In addition, five enabling conditions for collective teacher efficacy are identified and explained.

When forming judgments about their future capabilities, teams draw on previous experiences. Bandura (1993) noted that efficacy beliefs evolve based on four types of past experiences: mastery experiences, vicarious experiences, social persuasion, and affective states (Figure 1.6). Results from past performances are the primary source of efficacy-shaping information for individuals and teams. Previous firsthand experiences provide teams with authentic evidence of whether or not they have what it takes to succeed (Bandura, 1993). When teams meet with success (mastery experiences), they come to expect that they can repeat successful performances. "Success raises mastery expectations" (Bandura, 1977, p. 195). Efficacy and achievement alternate as causes and effects. As a sense of efficacy results in increased performance, better performance outcomes further strengthen collective efficacy, which results in additional increases in performance. On the other hand, when teams do not succeed, repeated failure becomes a source of diminishing efficacy, especially when experienced early on (Bandura, 1977).

Figure 1.6   A Model for Leading Collective Teacher Efficacy: Sources of Efficacy Beliefs

SUPPORTIVE

Goal Consensus

Embedded Reflective Practices

MASTERY EXPERIENCES • VICARIOUS EXPERIENCES • SOCIAL PERSUASION • AFFECTIVE STATES •

Collective Teacher Efficacy

Empowered Teachers

Cohesive Teacher Knowledge

LEADERSHIP

Source: Based on research conducted by Bandura (1977).

In schools, an indicator of educators' previous success would include students' prior academic achievement. The greater the increase in students' achievement, the more successful experience a faculty has to draw upon as a basis for developing collective efficacy. This is what Denise Cleary (acting superintendent) in Linden Public Schools knew when she asked Derek Kondratowicz, the district data and assessment supervisor, to share data that showed significant improvement in academic achievement in a number of grade levels with teachers during an after-school meeting. The data at Linden Public Schools showed a significant increase in achievement in many grade levels, and it also demonstrated that Grade 5 students outperformed the state in English Language Arts for the first time. After 3 years of intense work, Denise knew it would be empowering for teams to see how their efforts paid off and capitalized on the opportunity to use mastery experiences to further enhance collective efficacy in the district. Readers will learn more about the journey to success in Linden Public Schools in Chapter 3.

Knowing that drawing upon previous success in raising student achievement is one of the most effective ways to develop collective efficacy might be disheartening for some teams, especially in cases where students' prior academic achievement has remained low. If students' academic achievement has not yet increased, what are other sources that can be drawn upon to shape a team's future beliefs about what they are capable of accomplishing? Vicarious experiences also have incredible power in harnessing collective efficacy. Collective efficacy increases when teams learn that others, faced with similar challenges, met with success (Bandura, 1986). This was Principal D'Les Gonzales Herron's experience in San Antonio during the Opening Classroom Doors initiative. While participating in the leadership network of the 20-school cohort, she had the opportunity to visit, collect data, and make improvement suggestions during Instructional Rounds in her colleagues' schools. D'Les's school, Briscoe Elementary, didn't host visitors until several years into the initiative but that didn't mean that D'Les wasn't learning and making improvements. By the time Briscoe hosted the Opening Classroom Doors visit, the staff were well on their way to transforming their school. Vicarious experiences in other schools and other classrooms impacted their work. The Briscoe Elementary team's efficacy was enhanced early on because they saw other teachers in the district succeeding under similar circumstances. Readers will learn more about Briscoe Elementary's story in Chapter 4.

"Seeing people similar to oneself succeed by perseverant effort raises observers' beliefs about their own abilities" (Bandura, 1998, p. 54).

Social persuasion is the third source of efficacy-shaping information. This happens when teams are convinced to take risks and told that they have what it takes to accomplish their goals. Social persuasion is a form of influence that is exercised when a credible and trustworthy colleague convinces a group that they constitute an effective team. Bandura (1998) noted that "effective efficacy builders do more than convey positive appraisals. They structure situations for others in ways that bring success and avoid placing them, prematurely, in situations where they are likely to fail" (p. 54). Ken Wallace, superintendent at Maine Township High School District in Illinois, knew this as he built a leadership team of social persuaders. Ken noted that building a team of persuaders "who agreed something needed to change allowed for the message to be filtered to all educators from multiple levels." With a rapidly changing shift in demographics (increased enrollment of students from low socioeconomic backgrounds), it was important to help teams in Maine Township see themselves as capable of meeting the learning needs of all students. Readers will learn more about Maine Township's success in overcoming challenges, including restricted access to enriched programs, in Chapter 2.

The final source of efficacy-shaping information that comes from past experiences is what Bandura (1998) called affective states. Affective states refers to the intensity in which individuals and teams experience feelings as they step outside their comfort zones. Risk can invoke worry, concern, anxiety, and insecurity to name a few negative feelings that teams might experience. On the other hand, when teams experience positive feelings associated with the work of school improvement, it results in an increased sense of collective efficacy. Positive feelings include optimism, hope, and pride. Readers will learn how Garth Larson, former principal at Butte des Morts Elementary School, instilled a sense of optimism, hope, and pride in the staff in order to develop collective teacher efficacy in Chapter 5.

> "Positive mood enhances a sense of efficacy" (Bandura, 1998, p. 54).

Five Enabling Conditions for Collective Teacher Efficacy

In addition to Bandura's (1998) sources of efficacy that are based on past experiences, research studies (Adams & Forsyth, 2006; Ross et al., 2004) also demonstrated the theoretical relevance of *contextual factors* (here and now factors) as additional and significant efficacy-shaping sources in schools. As noted earlier, each chapter of this book highlights one of the enabling conditions (Figure 1.7) that have been identified through research as malleable, contextual antecedents of collective teacher efficacy. While enabling conditions do not *cause* things to happen, they increase the likelihood that things will turn out as expected. These enabling conditions are Goal Consensus,

> Adams and Forsyth (2006) differentiated between two types of sources of collective efficacy. The criterion they used to differentiate was in relation to the "proximity of occurrence to present teaching realities by which efficacy sources exist" (p. 630). They called for a need to classify mastery experiences, vicarious experiences, social persuasion, and affective states as "remote" sources because "they occurred at some time in the past" (p. 630) and present contextual conditions as "proximate" sources because they "have a day in and day out influence on the teaching tasks" (p. 630).

Figure 1.7   A Model for Leading Collective Teacher Efficacy

In Jenni's earlier book, *Collective Efficacy: How Educators' Beliefs Impact Student Learning* (2017), Jenni identified six enabling conditions for collective efficacy. Recently, Jenni, along with O'Leary and Hattie (2020), conducted a study to produce a questionnaire to measure the enabling conditions for collective teacher efficacy. The design and validation of the scale included statistical techniques (exploratory and confirmatory factor analysis) to determine composite reliability of the enabling conditions. Based on this analysis (from both a technical and theoretical perspective), the Enabling Conditions for Collective Teacher Efficacy Scale (EC-CTES) contained the following five subscales: Goal Consensus, Empowered Teachers, Cohesive Teacher Knowledge, Empowered Teachers, Cohesive Teacher Knowledge, Embedded Reflective Practices, and Supportive Leadership (Donohoo, O'Leary, & Hattie, 2020).

Goal Consensus

Goal setting is part of a cycle of evidence-based assessment, analysis, and determination of next steps (Robinson, Hohepa, & Lloyd, 2009). There is a strong relationship between goal consensus and collective teacher efficacy (Kurz & Knight, 2003; Ross et al., 2004). In schools with high levels of understanding and consensus around goals, school-wide improvement goals are clear, specific, and realistic. Improvement goals are established and understood by all teaching staff, and there is a process in place for teachers to collaborate when setting goals for improvement. Readers will learn how superintendent Ken Wallace and his team at Maine Township built consensus around goals in Chapter 2.

Empowered Teachers

When the conditions are set for teachers to come together to determine solutions to challenges of practices and hierarchy is flattened, it helps foster a sense of collective efficacy. Empowering teachers (promoting teacher leadership and influence within the school) has been deemed important, as past research has identified the strong and positive relationship between teacher influence (Goddard, 2002; Ross et al., 2004), teacher leadership (Derrington & Angelle, 2013), and collective teacher efficacy. In Chapter 3, readers will learn how Linden Public Schools in New Jersey strengthened collective efficacy and ultimately increased student achievement by empowering teachers.

Cohesive Teacher Knowledge

Embedded Reflective Practices, and Supportive Leadership. It isn't our intention to inundate readers with the statistical details of the study. We did feel it was important, however, to explain the reason for the revisions to the original list of enabling conditions that was published in 2017. Additional information regarding the design and validation of the EC-CTES can be found in Appendix B and at http://teacher-efficacy.com/our_services/enabling-conditions/.

Ross and colleagues' (2004) research identified that goal setting had a stronger effect on collective teacher efficacy than prior student achievement.

In 2002, Goddard found that an increase of one standard deviation in collective teacher efficacy was associated with a 0.41 standard deviation increase in teacher influence. Where teachers had the opportunity to influence important, instructionally relevant school decisions, they also tended to have stronger beliefs in the combined ability of the faculty to positively impact student achievement.

Cohesion is defined as the degree to which teachers agree with each other about what constitutes effective assessment and instructional practices. Ross et al. (2004) found the more cohesive the faculty, the more likely they were to be influenced by social persuasion. The researchers believed the reason for this was because the more cohesive the staff, the more likely they would be aware of each other's concerns. The awareness of concerns was then useful in building persuasive arguments about the important role that individuals contributed to the team. Ross et al. (2004) further pointed out that the greater the cohesion, the more opportunities teachers had to experience successful collaboration, and the "social

Opening Classroom Doors is a process similar to Instructional Rounds in Education (City, Elmore, Fiarman, & Teitel, 2009) but modified for local contextual needs and enhanced with new approaches from data team and coaching traditions.

processes that generated peer support were likely to reduce the effects of negative emotions on collective efficacy beliefs" (p. 167). Readers will learn how D'Les Gonzales Herron, former principal at Briscoe Elementary, helped build cohesive teacher knowledge through the process of Opening Classroom Doors in Chapter 4.

Embedded Reflective Practices

Embedded reflective practices are processes by which teams work together to examine sources of student evidence to help inform their work. "When instructional improvement efforts result in improved student outcomes that are validated through sources of student learning data, educators' collective efficacy is strengthened. Evidence of collective impact, in turn, reinforces proactive collective behaviors, feelings, thoughts, and motivations" (Donohoo, Hattie, & Eells, 2018, p. 42). Embedded reflection in light of evidence helps to uncover cause-and-effect relationships (quality teaching causes student learning) and would therefore highlight firsthand mastery experiences and vicarious experiences for teacher teams. Teachers come to realize the positive results of their own efforts, others' efforts, and their combined efforts through processes that enable embedded reflective practices. Embedded reflective practices are at the heart of teachers' collaborative work. Teachers become empowered, build consensus on goals, and develop greater cohesion when reflection in light of student evidence is embedded in their common practices. Readers will learn about strategies and tools to embed reflective practice in Chapter 5.

Supportive Leadership

Supportive leadership centers upon the school leadership's approach to buffering teachers from distractions and the recognition of individual and team accomplishments. It goes beyond that, however, in the sense that leaders play an important role in nurturing the conditions for the other enabling conditions to be realized as well. School leaders establish the processes and procedures that help to *empower teachers* and ensure that teachers are regularly *reflecting* on their practice in light of evidence. They create the conditions to foster collaboration, increase teachers' knowledge of each other's work, and build greater *cohesion* amongst their staff. They can also establish a process for gaining *consensus on school goals*. Readers will learn more about the role of supportive leadership in developing collective teacher efficacy in Chapter 6.

What is important to note is that these five enabling conditions are malleable—they can be molded, modified, and changed. They are within a leader's scope of influence. There are other contextual factors that influence collective teacher efficacy that are out of the leader's and faculty's control. Bandura (1993) and Hoy, Smith, and Sweetland (2003) demonstrated that students' socioeconomic status influenced collective teacher efficacy. We are not here to argue that socioeconomic status doesn't matter. Hattie's (2019) Visible Learning® research synthesis, the largest research database that examines factors that influence student achievement, demonstrates that socioeconomic status has an effect size of 0.52. While low socioeconomic status is likely to negatively influence student achievement, collective teacher efficacy is more powerful, with an effect size of 1.39 (Hattie, 2019). Bandura (1993) demonstrated that the effect of collective teacher efficacy on student achievement was stronger than the link between socioeconomic status and student achievement. Goddard et al. (2017) demonstrated that collective efficacy closes achievement gaps. What is most important is that educators realize they hold the power to address issues of inequity when they intentionally build collective efficacy.

Goddard, Goddard, Kim, and Miller (2015) examined the relationships among leadership, teacher collaboration, collective efficacy, and student achievement and found that the more robust the sense of collective efficacy, "the greater their levels of student achievement, even after controlling for school and student background characteristics and prior levels of student achievement" (p. 525).

An effect size emphasizes the difference in magnitude of different factors for the purpose of comparison. An effect size of 0 reveals that the influence had no effect on student achievement. The larger the effect size, the more powerful the influence. Hattie (2009) suggested that an effect size of 0.20 is relatively small, an effect size of 0.40 is medium, and an effect size of 0.60 is large.

Sandoval, Challoo, and Kupczynski (2011) examined the relationship between collective teacher efficacy and student achievement at economically disadvantaged middle school campuses and found that the efficacious campuses could impact student achievement through their belief in their colleagues' ability to impact student achievement regardless of the students' background and socioeconomic status.

Powerful stories provide inspiration as well as information to educators seeking to build collective efficacy in their own schools.

Conclusion

In this chapter, we compared and contrasted a team who lacked collective efficacy with a team whose efficacy was firmly established and considered the consequences of both. We explored how efficacy beliefs drive receptiveness to change. We also demonstrated how a team's future-oriented efficacy beliefs are influenced based on both *past experiences* and *current contextual factors*. In the chapters that follow, we share stories from leaders in education who have been successful in increasing student achievement and addressed issues of inequity by enabling the conditions in which collective efficacy is enhanced. These powerful stories provide inspiration as well as information to educators seeking to build collective efficacy in their own schools.

Goal Consensus 2

The Nature of Goal Consensus

Listening to David Snowden, a revered researcher in the field of knowledge management, Stef was taken aback when Snowden (2020) stated unequivocally, "there is no such thing as goal consensus." As he spoke, Stef gradually realized that he was using the term *consensus* as synonymous with *unanimous*. In reading other researchers around this topic, this appears to be a fairly common practice, and one that might undermine our ability to embrace goal consensus as a critical element of building collective efficacy.

The *Cambridge Dictionary* defines consensus as "a generally accepted opinion; wide agreement," whereas unanimity is defined as "complete agreement among every member of a group." While the distinction may be subtle, it is important not to conflate consensus as unanimous agreement and it is equally important not to insist on unanimity before moving forward or we would doom every initiative before it begins.

> Goal consensus is reached when the faculty that has engaged in a process for identifying goals comes to an agreement about the school's goals.

Another nuanced challenge in understanding the nature of goal consensus is that groups rarely work toward one single intention. In our increasingly complex world, challenges are not met with one simple (or even complicated) goal. Instead, groups must determine the overarching goal that drives the need for their work together, they must consider the smaller purpose-driven goals that will guide their work in a coherent fashion, and they must distinguish between mastery and performance goals to motivate teams and increase goal-relevant behaviors. In a sense, groups might find more success achieving goal consensus if they approach it as a collaborative process rather than an action to accomplish.

In addition to these challenges, goals must not be considered sacrosanct, as if they were etched in stone. As teams progress along their learning journey, they must be willing to revisit, revise, and rethink their goals in light of new understandings. Sometimes the most important thing we learn is that we were heading down the wrong path all along.

VIGNETTE 2.1

Goal Consensus as a Reflective Practice

The leadership team in Maine Township knew they needed to do something to shift the focus away from teacher-centered classrooms. As one administrator put it, "Every time I walked into a classroom, it was clear where the focal point was—the front of the room. When an adult opened the door to visit the class, every student swiveled their head to turn and see who had entered."

The team believed that cooperative learning skills were sorely needed. They decided to invest in a robust "train the trainer" model, embarking on an initiative that would theoretically result in training all of the Maine Township educators in cooperative learning strategies. Well into the implementation, the leadership team noticed something that became a great source of frustration: the only classrooms where there was a demonstrated shift in practice were those whose teachers had begun training colleagues following the "train the trainer" session. It wasn't spreading out to the other educators in the buildings.

This raised two critical questions for the leadership team: how can we create skill-learning opportunities that move beyond the traditional "one-off" workshop so they actually change instructional practice? The other question came from the observation that those teachers who had stepped up to become trainers were clearly most invested in changing the learning for students. Therefore, how might Maine

Township create more opportunities for teachers to take on those leadership roles?

The leadership team realized that while their original goal focused on shifting practice to create more student-centered classrooms is worthy, it didn't direct them in a way that would actually result in changes to the student learning experience. They realized that the more critical goals to pursue revolved around adult learning. The Maine Township leadership team developed a new theory of action: Shifting the goal to one that creates optimal conditions for teachers to learn—focusing on adults—would have a higher likelihood in changing practice, thus impacting the student learning experience.

Source: Maine Township, District 207. Used with permission.

The importance of goal consensus in building collective efficacy has been highlighted throughout the last decades. Kurz and Knight (2003) found that consensus on school goals was a significant predictor of collective efficacy. Robinson et al.'s research (2009) on the impacts of leadership identified five powerful leadership dimensions, one of which was establishing goals and expectations. Most notable about their description was the need for staff involvement in order to provide clarity and consensus around goals. In *District Leadership That Works: Striking the Right Balance*, Marzano and Waters recognized that collaborative goal setting has been noted in the research for at least 40 years, and they wrote that book in 2009!

The importance of goal consensus is a deceptively simple concept. In reality, achieving goal consensus requires leadership and a commitment of time and resources. It also requires a careful understanding of the nature of goals. Goal consensus does not mean that a group will work toward a single, definitive end game. Figuring out what an organization's goals should be is a challenging process; while it may seem like the logical first step in any initiative, goals often reveal themselves along the journey. As Jill Geocaris, the Innovative Adult Learning coordinator from Maine Township, described, "We did a lot of finding our way during the first two years. It wasn't that there was a lack of goals—we had a clear vision of learning from the superintendent, we had areas of focus—and then we realized that we had to pull things together for people because they weren't seeing how everything was connected. It's not that the goals were wrong, it's that organizations reflect and refresh every once in a while."

The Maine Township Journey

Superintendent Ken Wallace faced a dilemma: his district of three high schools was experiencing a rapidly changing student population and educators were clinging to outdated teaching approaches. Ken reflected, "It was difficult to come in and uncover what was happening. We weren't meeting student needs especially in the area of access. Our most challenging courses too often weren't available to our traditionally underserved students, a population that has been our fastest growing. It would have been easier to maintain the status quo—identifying the need and bringing it out in the open was a tremendous risk."

A critical first move was to build a leadership team composed of believers; it was important that the school leaders agreed that something needed to change. Building this team was important because it allowed for messages of change to filter to all educators from multiple levels, not just the superintendent's office. In this respect, the leadership team was very intentional in using social persuasion as an efficacy enhancer. The team knew that the changes required would leave some people feeling uneasy, anxious, or even inadequate. This recognition is an important aspect of any implementation and is particularly crucial when considering educators' receptiveness to change (Figure 2.1). The team recognized that starting out, teachers might dismiss or evade proposed changes, as is often the case in the early stages of implementation

Figure 2.1 Receptiveness to Change During Stages of Implementation Matrix

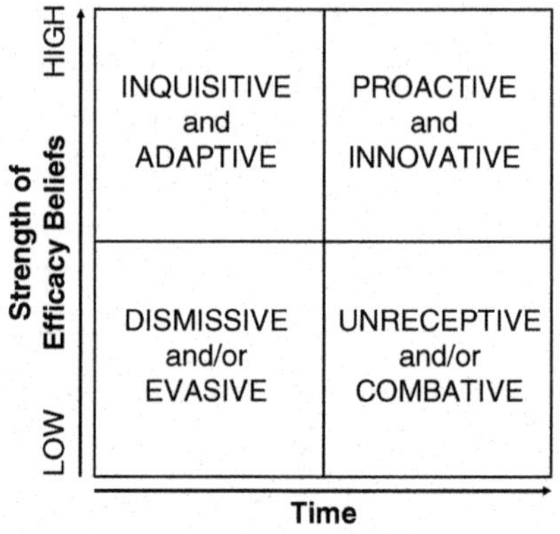

where efficacy beliefs are not strong. Without significant support, those beliefs might continue to be low. Over time, this might result in educators continuing to resist or, worse, becoming combative. To address the receptiveness issue, Ken intentionally strove to minimize concerns by communicating high standards while providing assurances "*we know you can do this* and we're here to support you."

The leadership team noticed the greatest impediment to student success was restricted access; the most successful students were those who had access to the most enriched programs. And yet, that access was denied to many students—particularly minority students—and the team viewed this as a fundamental system design flaw. Their steady insistence on creating more access for greater numbers of students became the mission. The issue of access to advanced coursework is not unique to Maine Township. "Too many Black, Latino, and low-income students . . . are not given the chance to participate in advanced coursework or programs in high school . . . . These students are missing out on critical opportunities that can set them up for success in college and careers" (Education Trust, 2019).

Believing that access alone would not be enough to support students— particularly those with little experience in rigorous courses—Maine Township also pursued new teaching methodologies. An additional goal was developed, to shift instruction from the traditional style prevalent in many classrooms. With this intention, Maine Township educators were acknowledging what Martin Haberman (1991) described as the "pedagogy of poverty"—teacher-centric practices based heavily on passivity and compliance. "Such experiences are too commonly sustained in our current educational system, where teacher preparation programs often fail to support educators in developing the skills and mindsets needed to close the opportunity and achievement gaps of struggling students" (Riordan, Klein, & Gaynor, 2019, p. 327). A recognition of these two barriers to student success—access and pedagogy—represented a radical shift in district goals.

As the district attempted various approaches to supporting both teachers and students, they pursued the "train the trainer" model to implement cooperative learning practices and discovered an implementation gap—the "one-stop workshop" wasn't effective. As a result, they moved to professional learning designs that would permit more embedded and meaningful learning experiences. Maine Township's focus on student success wasn't misplaced; it was the ultimate long-term goal. They learned that they needed to consider and articulate more immediate benchmark goals that would move them on their journey.

Focusing on Adult Learning

The Maine Township district website clearly states, "Adult learning is at the foundation of student learning in our district." The professional learning program was thoughtfully constructed with a focus on coaching. Maine Township first learned from educational coaching experts and then made a conscious decision to break from a fundamental belief in the field—that you shouldn't *make* people participate in coaching. This was a significant challenge and caused some pushback. The leadership team held their ground, however, believing that the only way to achieve a tipping point in practice was to acknowledge that coaching is good for everyone, not just those who see the need.

The adult learning program in Maine Township identified learning pathways to define how educators would meet the academic and social/emotional needs of students. Those pathways were closely aligned to district beliefs about the student learning and experiences that would support their future to success. A fundamental value in Maine Township is that high expectations for changes in educator beliefs and practice demand a high level of support in the form of time and resources, opportunities for individuals and teams to experience mastery, and efficacy-enhancing feedback through coaching. This required implementing a multitiered support system, with beliefs about what students need connecting to adult learning goals in a reciprocal relationship.

Focusing on the adults as a way to address inequity and instructional improvement is far from the norm. As noted by Hammond (2015), "Too often we focus only on doing something to culturally and linguistically diverse students without changing ourselves, especially when our students are dependent learners who are not able to access their full academic potential on their own" (p. 52). The emphasis on adult learning was a bold move by Maine Township to confront inequities that existed in their system.

Overcoming Challenges

The Maine Township leadership team acknowledged that it was not a linear trajectory of success in their approach to adult learning. Jill Geocaris described a significant missed opportunity: when initially rolling out the coaching model, the district invested a lot of time and resources into training the coaches, assuming that the staff *being coached* didn't need any training at all. "It was as if we trained the coaches behind a veil of secrecy," Jill reflected, "and it would have really helped those first coaches if we had thought to train the staff." The staff is now "there" in terms of their willingness and openness to the coaching model, but Jill acknowledged that the initial effort probably took a lot more time than it should have. While Maine Township certainly explained the program and why it was important, the extra step that Jill wishes they had taken would have supported staff in understanding how to get the most out of their work with the coaches.

Interestingly, the district recently embarked on a new coaching model for cooperating teachers working with preservice education students. Jill laughingly observed, "You think we would have learned, but we did it again! We trained the cooperating teachers on how to work with novices but didn't train the preservice teachers." After the first year of implementation, the cooperating teachers noted that student teachers should have been involved in the coaching training. Jill wryly noted, "Maybe the third time will be the charm!"

This implementation gap lesson was clearly learned because the adjustment was made for year two of the program. Now the cooperating teachers and student teachers are trained in coaching methodologies together. It is having an impact as evidenced in this quote from one of the cooperating teachers: "It's not as if I wouldn't have had some of these conversations with [my student teacher] without what we did [in this program]. But it's more intentional. There's a little bit more structure to it, and I feel a little bit more accountable to it. And so, you add all those things together, it's made it smoother, it's made it more organized. It's been a more positive experience for me; I think I've grown more because of it."

Evidence of Success

Since fully implementing the adult learning initiative, Maine Township has seen significant increases in student achievement on various measures. One of their significant goals was to increase access for students to enriched programs and higher-level courses. From 2008 to 2020 (Figure 2.2), enrollment in accelerated, dual credit, or advanced

Figure 2.2   Maine Township Course Enrollment Trend

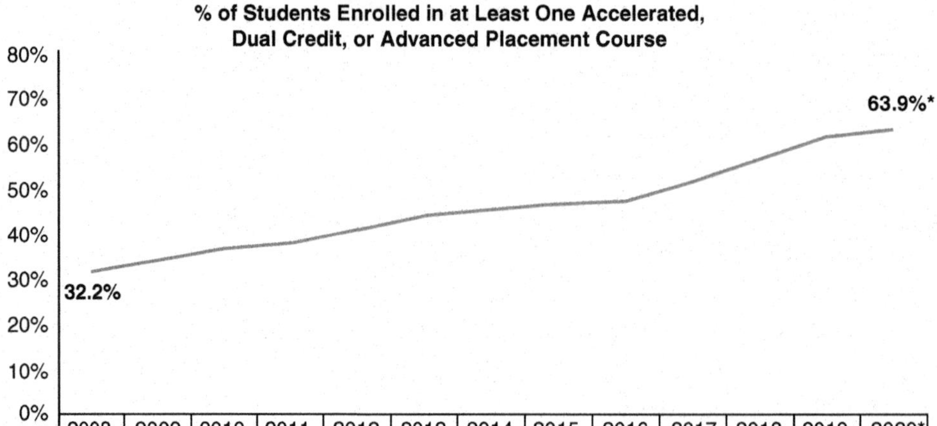

% of Students Enrolled in at Least One Accelerated, Dual Credit, or Advanced Placement Course

	2008	2009	2010	2011	2012	2013	2014	2015	2016	2017	2018	2019	2020*
——Acc+DC=AP	32.2%	34.7%	37.3%	38.9%	41.6%	44.6%	45.8%	47.5%	48.1%	52.7%	57.7%	62.1%	63.9%

63.9%*

32.2%

Source: Maine Township, District 207. Used with permission.

*2020 figure is projected enrollment.

placement courses almost doubled, demonstrating that the removal of barriers and increases in support had the desired effect on student access.

An additional measure of success in Maine Township is student performance on the ACT (a university entrance exam). While the student population had shifted to one composed of more students from low socioeconomic environments, that same population significantly improved their performance on the ACT measure (Figure 2.3). The black line indicates a linear regression calculation of what would have happened to the mean if nothing else had changed, particularly in Maine Township's instructional program. The top green line indicates the actual ACT performance, showing a 0.9 higher mean in 2017 over 2002, when universal ACT testing began. The 22.6 mean of 2017 is 3.4 points higher than what would have been predicted, based on the low-income increase. After 7 years of significant work on goal alignment and adult learning, Maine Township students outperform based on predicted composite scores. Given that the ACT composite scores are typically 23.6 for higher income and 19.5 for lower income students, this is a powerful closing of the income achievement gap (Mattern, Radunzel, & Harmston, 2016).

Determining student achievement is a difficult part of the work, particularly when there is controversy over which assessments are meaningful measures of success. Illinois state assessments have been recognized as containing "significant racial and class bias" (Feagin & Barnett, 2004).

Figure 2.3   Maine Township Percentage of Free and Reduced-Price Lunch and Average ACT

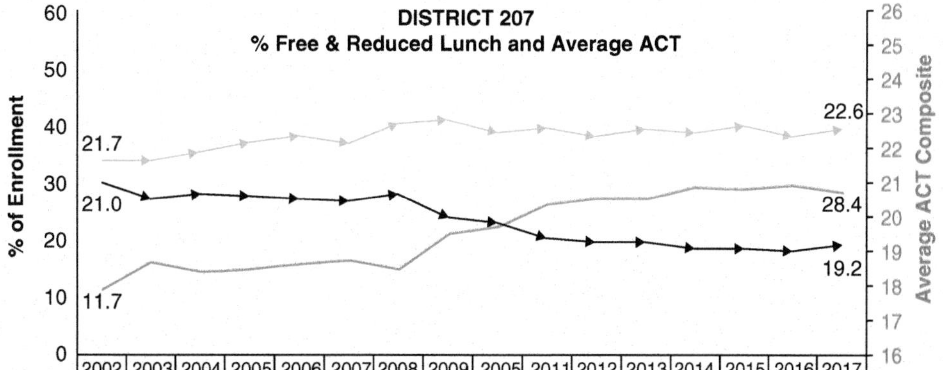

	2002	2003	2004	2005	2006	2007	2008	2009	2005	2011	2012	2013	2014	2015	2016	2017
DISTRICT 207 % FRL	11.7	16.2	14.5	14.2	16.1	16.6	14.9	21.1	22.4	26.5	27.4	27.4	29.4	29.1	29.7	28.4
Avg.ACT Composite	21.7	21.7	21.9	22.2	22.4	22.2	22.8	22.2	22.5	22.6	22.4	22.6	22.5	22.7	22.4	22.6
Predict.ACT Composite	21.0	20.5	20.7	20.6	20.5	20.5	20.7	20.0	19.8	19.4	19.3	19.3	19.1	19.1	19.0	19.2

Source: Maine Township, District 207. Used with permission.

Nevertheless, student performance on those assessments was used to criticize the work in districts like Maine Township (Johnson, 2019). Collective efficacy among educators supports their ability to stay the course and persist, particularly when controversy arises over what measures to use. Superintendent Ken Wallace affirms, "In perhaps the most important areas, like career advisement and exploration, the reports [from state assessments] are years behind in their ability to reflect what actually matters to students, parents and communities. We will continue to work toward designing schools that meet the needs of every learner so that we focus on our students' abilities to succeed well beyond high school." Meeting the challenge of implicit bias in standardized testing requires continuous embedded reflection on the equity goals established by a school district.

It is also important to recognize other success criteria besides data points from assessment results. Recalling the story of overwhelmingly teacher-centered classrooms, which prompted the initial investment in cooperative learning, Jill Geocaris noted, "Back then, every head would swivel when an adult would walk into the classroom during a lesson. It's completely different now: when I walk into a class, no one even looks up. The students are so engaged in what they are learning and discussing together—they don't even notice when I enter the room!" There are tangible signs that coaching has impacted instructional practices to such an extent, the entire student experience has shifted.

Another important sign of success comes from the numbers of applications to leadership roles and positions in the district. By strategically creating more and more leadership opportunities for teachers, more and more educators are involved in the various focus committees, whether it be literacy, social-emotional learning, technology, differentiated instruction, and more. When the original coaching positions were posted, the applicants were from the core group of educators described as "the usual suspects," or the teachers that would typically volunteer for leadership roles. Over the years, an increase in leadership opportunities for educators has affected the applicant pool. During the most recent round of applications, "new" people applied, notably, those who were recently engaged in some type of leadership activity. The leadership experience provides educators with a "hook" as they begin to see the connectedness of district goals for students and adult learning competencies. It is natural that they then want to support their colleagues to also see that connectedness.

The adult learning priority is completely transparent to the school community; students are well aware of teachers who have participated and the difference it makes in their practice. As one teacher put it, "It's pretty humbling when an 11th grader asks if you've had a chance yet to be involved in a coaching experience."

How Does Goal Consensus Develop Collective Efficacy?

In this chapter, our focus is on goal consensus (Figure 2.4). Maine Township's consensus on a series of goals impacts multiple elements that have been shown to increase collective efficacy. The adult learning pathways combined with coaching create multiple opportunities for mastery experiences. When teachers try new approaches to instruction and those approaches resonate with students, they naturally want to continue their efforts.

In Maine Township, one of the driving goals is to create as many leadership opportunities for teachers as possible. These opportunities to work meaningfully on a team create leadership opportunities that traditionally haven't existed for many teachers. When those leadership opportunities are available—along with the time and resources to do the work—it builds collective efficacy. The significant emphasis on creating opportunities via committees and peer coaching provides educators with critical

Figure 2.4   A Model for Leading Collective Efficacy: Goal Consensus

opportunities to collaborate around a focused goal. Importantly, teachers are not only leading the development (via the committees) but are front and center in coaching their colleagues. Their learnings and successes create frequent opportunities for vicarious experiences.

By involving teachers directly with each other in the form of coaching, there are significant opportunities for interdependent work. Coaches and teachers collaborate on a point of inquiry that is immediately relevant because it is based on an individual teacher's context and student need. Working to investigate and strategize around that point of inquiry is a prime example of professional interdependence. When teachers are successful as a result of their coaching, they enjoy another opportunity for a mastery experience on two levels: one for the teacher who successfully implemented a new instructional strategy and one for the coach who successfully supported a colleague in their work.

The nested series of goals Maine Township has set provide guidance and coherence to the work they are undertaking. Yes, the overarching vision is student success—and that is supported by a series of clear and coherent adult learning goals aligned to a clear vision of what student success actually means in Maine Township. The leadership team's willingness to revisit and course correct—with stakeholder involvement—is the process that embodies goal consensus.

When organizing a retreat for staff members involved in adult learning leadership roles in the district, one of the teacher leaders expressed surprise that there were so many names on the invitation list. Jill Geocaris quipped, "I'm building an army!" The process has truly built a sense of belonging through slow and steady insistence on all educators aspiring to reach the competencies that have been set for all learners in the community—adults as well as students.

How Can We Support Goal Consensus in Our School or District?

In terms of reaching goal consensus, it is important to remember the examples presented earlier in this chapter. Goal consensus is more of a process toward common understanding than it is an attempt to reach unanimity. The term *shared vision* has long been used by change theorists, and this may be a helpful way to consider goal consensus. In *Taking Charge of Change*, Hord, Rutherford, Huling-Austin, and Hall (2014) explain, "We recommend the development of a shared vision, or mental image, of what the change will look like when it has been implemented well and is operational. . . . Having a picture in the "mind's eye" of the change in operation provides the implementer with a target for initiating the work to be done to reach full implementation of the change" (p. 76). Leaders must consider how to create transparency and clarity in creating a shared vision and how best to achieve consensus around making the vision a reality. There are many ways to approach the process of goal consensus, and it begins with a leader acknowledging their own role with some humility and willingness to make it a collaborative team effort.

Research and psychology provide insights into how goal setting works and why goal setting is important. In the section that follows, we summarize some of the important ideas gleaned from researchers and psychologists. When helping teams gain consensus on goals, it's important for leaders to

- obtain input from various stakeholders in developing a shared vision;

- know the difference between mastery and performance goals;

- identify long-term, mid-journey, and small-win goals; and

- motivate persistent goal-oriented behavior.

Obtain Input From Various Stakeholders in Developing a Shared Vision

Collaborating to develop a shared vision requires all stakeholder voices to be heard, and this can feel overwhelming when groups are large and perhaps geographically widespread. Recently, Stef was asked to help facilitate gathering data from stakeholders to support vision refinement of a statewide initiative involving hundreds of participants in far-flung locations. Stef's team used a stakeholder interview process popular in UX (user experience) design. Over the course of several sessions, large groups were gathered and participants were asked to self-organize into triads. Within a triad, each stakeholder played each role: the interviewer, the interviewee, and the note-taker. Responding to a series of guided questions posed by the interviewer, each interviewee responded with stories, insights, hopes, and concerns. Note-takers gathered the information in a prepared template. The process repeated until every participant had a chance to share their thinking. The notes from all interviews were compiled and processed by the team to find commonalities, ultimately creating a concept map representing the system's vision as a whole. While an intensive undertaking, the stakeholder interviews perform a critical function during the initial stages of a goal consensus process: every voice was heard so that when the ultimate vision was shared, each participant recognized their part in creating it. (More information about conducting stakeholder interviews can be found in Appendix C.) The test for whether a vision is truly shared by all may best be described by Senge, Cambron-McCabe, Lucas, and Smith (2012), who wrote, "A vision is not really shared unless it has staying power and an evolving life force that lasts for years, propelling people through a continuous cycle of action, learning, and reflection" (p. 87).

When an overarching vision has been established, mastery and performance goals (long-term, mid-journey, and small-win goals) can be identified. These goals should not be etched in stone but be subject to frequent scrutiny, consideration, and revision as needed. As Wheatley (2006) wrote, "We need to be able to

Robinson et al. (2009) noted that the degree of staff consensus about school goals was a significant discriminator between otherwise similar high- and low-performing schools in their meta-analysis on the impact of leadership on student outcomes.

trust that something as simple as a clear core of values and vision, kept in motion through dialogue, can lead to order" (p. 147). The larger vision acts as a container; within the container, members of the system can develop and work toward goals aligned with the vision.

Know the Difference Between Mastery and Performance Goals

When building consensus on goals, it is important to note the difference between mastery and performance goals and what that difference means in relation to motivating teams. In his book, *Drive: The Surprising Truth About What Motivates Us* (2009), Pink explores the often counterintuitive notions about motivation. When it comes to goals, Pink writes simply, "Goals work. The academic literature shows that by helping us tune out distractions, goals can get us to try harder, work longer, and achieve more" (p. 48). But delving more deeply into the nature of goals, research suggests "goals that people set for themselves and that are devoted to attaining mastery are usually healthy. But goals imposed by others—sales targets, quarterly returns, standardized test scores, and so on—can sometimes have dangerous side effects" (p. 50).

> Performance goals are goals that are directly related to an outcome. For example, "All students will improve their Spanish by 5 percent as represented on the final exam." A mastery goal is when teams set out to become the best they can be on a single task. For example, "All students will become proficient in Spanish." Research shows that mastery goals are preferable because they spark internal motivation.

Pink goes on to describe several cases of extrinsic and performance-oriented goals backfiring because they extinguish intrinsic motivation, encourage cheating or shortcuts, and foster short-term thinking. Mastery goals, on the other hand, encourage inquiry, promote collaboration, and are intrinsically motivating.

Maine Township's adult learning competencies provide an example of mastery versus performance goal. As part of their "Build Learner Ownership" pathway, competency 5.2 states: "I can utilize routines and strategies to empower learners to set and monitor progress toward personal and academic goals; develop abilities to self-reflect and self-regulate; cultivate growth mindsets; and influence perceptions of self-efficacy and purpose" (Maine Township District 207, 2020). Contrast that with a performance-oriented goal that, instead of monitoring student progress toward an academic goal, might set a standardized assessment expectation, such as solve 80 percent of the problems correctly.

This example of a mastery goal is powerful for several reasons: It encourages striving toward a goal rather than showing competence. By being open-ended, it does not remove the adult learner from the process but encourages creative and, possibly, collaborative approaches. It also encourages a long-term approach that cultivates a disposition in the learner rather than a short-term fix, such as tips and tricks for getting more problems correct on a test. We are not suggesting that systems do away with performance goals. They are important in identifying patterns and trends for subgroups of students and improvement over time. We are suggesting, however, that in order to activate goal-oriented behavior and motivation amongst educators, that leaders help teams focus on mastery goals. After all, research shows that when a mastery goal is met, the performance goal takes care of itself (Hidi & Harackiewicz, 2000).

> Research shows that when a mastery goal is met, the performance goal takes care of itself (Hidi & Harackiewicz, 2000).

Identify Long-Term, Mid-Journey, and Small-Win Goals

We find sand dunes (Figure 2.5) to be a helpful analogy when further considering goals. Sand dunes, from far away, look like smooth, sculpted mountains. When you get a closer look at the sand, however, we can see that it is made up of granules that vary in shade and size. More startling, when we look at sand under a microscope, we learn that it is even more irregular and variable in shape and color. These three different representations of the same sand are similar to the way we must approach goals. We need long-term goals (far away sand dunes), mid-journey goals (the sand itself), and small-win goals (microscopic grains of sand). All three are critical to

- agree on what we all believe represents success,
- understand the benchmarks along the way to the agreed-upon success, and
- celebrate movement along the path with small wins that direct our course.

Long-term goals—those distant sand dunes—are motivational in nature. They help teams to understand the big picture, the reason why the work should be undertaken. Long-term goals help to reduce ambiguity, which can be a significant threat to collective efficacy. Maintaining a clear, long-term vision is critical to a team's ability to stay the course.

> Maintaining a clear, long-term vision is critical to a team's ability to stay the course.

Figure 2.5 Sand Analogy

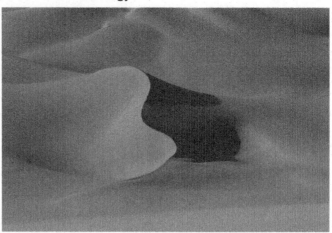

Image Sources: sand dunes from unsplash.com/audrius4x, sand close-up from unsplash
.com/@zedrex, sand under microscope from iStock.com/AlexmarPhoto

The mid-journey goals—those grains of sand—represent important benchmarks along the way. The magnitude of a long-term vision can be overwhelming, and so teams must establish markers of success in smaller, more manageable chunks. Just as important are the small-win goals that represent the day-to-day incremental work that moves educators along the path. These microscopic goals need to be celebrated as "wins" that provide teams with perspective on their progress and mastery and vicarious experiences. These experiences are essential in fostering belief among educators that they can do the hard work and see the impact of their efforts.

> Research shows that teachers' ambiguity and uncertainty impact their collective efficacy and, therefore, willingness to persevere against the challenges faced in schools today. Schechter and Qadach (2012) conducted a study with 801 elementary teachers and concluded that ambiguity was associated with a lack of efficacy.

> Goals that are attainable in a fairly short period of time focus attention on task-appropriate strategies through self-efficacy (Latham & Seijts, 1999).

Just as all stakeholders' voices shape the overarching vision, stakeholders must have the opportunity to come together for further consensus building about long-term, mid-journey, and small-win goals. One way to engage stakeholders in this process is through the co-creation of a logic model. A logic model is a tool that can be used to simplify complex relationships between various components for planning and monitoring progress. To aid in identifying the manageable chunks needed to achieve their goals, Maine Township used Killion's (2018) logic model to determine inputs, activities, outputs, and outcomes for both students in the system and adult professional learning.

Peter DeWitt (2020) described a logic model as "a concept map for leaders, teachers, and staff members to use as a means of working through the issues they seem to be facing" (p. 24). A typical logic model template (Appendix D) identifies an overarching mastery goal along with five categories—inputs, activities, initial outcomes (small-win goals), intermediate outcomes (mid-journey goals), and intended results (long-term performance goals). Killion (2008) noted that developing logic models are "collaborative efforts best done by a representative group of stakeholders" (p. 49). Leaders might enlist a design team to draft a logic model and then share the draft with additional stakeholders for

> Killion (2008) notes that one important aspect of a logic model is the identification of the ultimate goals of the organization.

their reaction and input. Logic models are then used by teams to monitor and revise goals accordingly.

Logic models help teams identify the overall mastery goal, along with the small-win, mid-journey, and long-term performance goals. Again, leaders are encouraged to activate goal-oriented behaviors by focusing teams' efforts on the mastery goal. The performance goal is important because it will provide systems with information about how subgroups of students are or are not progressing and, ultimately, provide insights about where resources are needed. However, the mastery goal is what will activate the team's efforts and persistence. An example of a partial logic model (Table 2.1) is provided on the facing page. A logic model template is also provided in Appendix D.

Logic models help teams take the overall vision and begin to think about the specific resources, activities, and intended outcomes or goals they hope to achieve. They are useful tools for building consensus on goals, laying out the actions necessary to achieve goals, and making stakeholders' long-term vision more transparent. We have noticed, however, that after teams create logic models, where they have trouble staying on top of monitoring progress toward their goals usually comes mid-journey. If mid-journey goals are not attained, the long-term goals will not be met. What's important is that leaders have teams continuously revisit their logic model in order to determine if goals are being met, or if they need to be revised, and to consider if additional resource "inputs" are needed.

We have found that a World Café protocol (Appendix E) has been useful in helping teams revisit logic models mid-journey, specifically to determine progress. The World Café is a flexible and effective format for hosting large group conversations. The facilitator provides a prompt and individuals join a group of their choosing and engage in free-flowing discussions. There are usually three prompts, revealed one at a time, over a 90-minute period. The conversations are captured in a variety of ways and can be analyzed for themes. This is the most critical aspect of the World Café because it reveals the patterns arising across the entire group's conversation. Capturing these emerging themes—whether they be concerns, celebrations, or ideas for refinement—allows all members of a team to have a voice in both reflecting on and revising the goals of their logic model. Although the World Café wasn't specifically designed for the use of revising logic models, when used with the right prompts it is an excellent way to access all voices and gain new

Table 2.1   Logic Model Example

Mastery Goal: Students will become proficient self-assessors who will be able to articulate where they are in relation to the learning intention and success criteria and use that information to determine next steps.				
Inputs	**Activities**	**Small-Win Goals**	**Mid-Journey Goals**	**Long-Term Performance Goals**
Full-time instructional coaches for each low-performing school and half-time coaches for middle- and high-performing schools.	Principals hire instructional coaches. Central office provides professional learning for coaches and coachees.	Coaches gain knowledge and skills for coaching teachers. Coaches gain access to classrooms and work with classroom teachers.	Coaches support teachers' engagement in collaborative inquiry. Coaches support implementation of learning intentions and success criteria.	Year 1: 60% of students score proficient or above on literacy and mathematics standardized tests. Most students are beginning to self-regulate their learning. Year 2: 80% of students score proficient or above on literacy and mathematics standardized tests. Many students possess the qualities of self-regulated learners. Year 3: 100% of students score proficient or above on literacy and mathematics standardized tests. All students become independent, self-regulated learners.
Human and fiscal resources to provide professional learning and follow-up support for classroom teachers.	Central office engages teams in collaborative inquiry designs for professional learning. Instructional coaches provide follow-up support for classroom implementation.	Teachers collaboratively identify learning intentions based on standards. Teachers construct success criteria and share them with students.	Teachers consistently share learning intentions with students. Teachers co-construct success criteria with students and have students interact with criteria in meaningful ways. Teachers have students self- and peer assess using success criteria.	
High-quality instruction for students.	Teachers use success criteria as the basis for effective feedback.	Students learn strategies for improving their performance based on self- and peer assessment.	Students apply the new strategies in their learning for both learning and pleasure.	

insights and consensus for goal setting. Readers will find examples of prompts and an outline of how to facilitate World Café in Appendix E.

Motivate Persistent, Goal-Oriented Behavior

It is one thing to create goals, but it is an entirely different thing to spark an urgency within teams to engage in the interdependent work necessary to accomplish goals. As noted earlier, small-win goals and mastery goals both help to motivate teams to accomplish goals. Another aspect of motivating teams to engage in the behaviors that will advance

"Differences between mental models explain why two people can observe the same event and describe it differently: They are paying attention to different details. The core task of the discipline of mental models is to bring tacit assumptions and attitudes to the surface so people can explore and talk about their differences and misunderstandings with minimal defensiveness. This process is crucial for people who want to understand their world, or their school, more completely—because, like a pane of glass framing and subtly distorting our vision, our mental models determine what we see . . . unexamined mental models limit people's ability to change" (Senge et al., 2012, pp. 99–100).

With student background factors controlled, leadership made a difference to students through the degree of emphasis on clear academic and learning goals (Robinson et al., 2009).

progress toward goals involves creating a discrepancy between where teams currently are and where they want to be.

This involves a two-part process. It first demands that teams accurately assess where they are in relation to the goals they set. And then it involves creating a dissatisfaction with the discrepancy between these two places that serves as an incentive to achieve. The space between these two ideas is what Senge and colleagues (2012) describe as "creative tension." In seeking a resolution to that tension, teams become aware of opportunities that support the move from "what is" to "what could be." Leaders must create a discrepancy between current realities and desired futures by helping teams examine their mental models. Where there is a discrepancy between a school's current situation and their desired future, the dissatisfaction experienced by the team motivates them to take action—to close the gap—as long as they are committed to the goal. When Ken Wallace shared the data showing the limited access to high-quality instructional experiences for many Maine Township students, he provided clarity on "what is" happening for students. He then challenged community stakeholders to consider "what could be" by envisioning a district that addresses inequity by creating access and opportunity for all students.

Conclusion

Goal consensus may seem like a deceptively simple concept until we consider it more as a process than a "thing" to accomplish. Keeping in mind the tiered nature of goals—long-term vision, mid-journey goals, and small-win goals—along with a framing in terms of mastery versus performance will help guide organizations to be highly intentional and widely inclusive in goal development. Ideally, an organization can point to a clear connection between small wins, mid-journey goals, and long-term vision. While it may seem a large challenge to create coherence between the various stakeholders in a system, they are bound together around the most important connection of all: their desire for the success of the students in their schools. Once that connection is made abundantly clear, building a shared vision is less daunting. Traditionally, the overarching vision has been determined by someone with an authoritative role—the superintendent, the school board, the principal. The need for vision to be developed collaboratively cannot be overstated. When based on authority alone, an imposed vision results in, at best, compliance, and, at worst, fractionalization and undermining behaviors. By encouraging participation from everyone within an organization, leadership is no longer a function of title or authority—everyone's voice is equally valid.

Goal consensus should be viewed as an ongoing and iterative process rather than seeking unanimity among stakeholders. As we saw with the Maine Township story, goals have multiple levels: the long-term vision that supports the journey, frequent checkpoints to assess progress, and short-term goals that make implementation manageable. In pursuit of developing goal consensus, we have to be willing to learn from mistakes by engaging groups in deep and meaningful reflection and being willing to make adjustments to our thinking. When groups are able to develop clear understandings around the purposes of their work, there is a higher likelihood that reflective practices will become regularly embedded in an ongoing effort to improve instruction. One such method of regularly revisiting goals is to structure a coherent system of adult learning directly tied to desired student achievement outcomes.

The need for vision to be developed collaboratively cannot be overstated.

3 Empowered Teachers

Teacher Leadership

Teacher leadership is not a new concept, but it has gained increasing attention in recent years. Traditionally, the role of teacher leaders has been an informal job title and limited by contextual factors such as school culture and administrative notions regarding teachers' work. For the most part, teachers who aspire to a leadership position in education have found very few options: either become a "master" or "mentor" teacher (traditionally based on years of experience) or leave teaching to pursue an administrative certificate (Livingston, 1992).

> Empowering teachers is about promoting teacher leadership and influence within the school. When the conditions are set for teachers to come together to determine solutions to challenges of practices and hierarchy is flattened, it helps in fostering a sense of collective efficacy.

More recently, the notion of teacher leadership has gained attention and rethinking in terms of what that role might encompass. With the publication of the Teacher Leader Model Standards in 2011 by a consortium of concerned educators, the term *teacher leader* has gained significant clarification. The standards organized the notion of teacher leadership around seven domains of practice: collaboration, research, professional learning, instruction, assessment, community outreach, and advocacy (Teacher Leadership Exploratory Consortium, 2017). In a recent study, Ingersoll, Dougherty, and Sirinides (2017) found that teachers infrequently wield school or district-wide leadership influence—but that "having a school improvement team that provides effective leadership and delegating a large role to teachers in this school improvement planning are among the most important school-based practices associated with improved student achievement" (p. 26). Figure 3.1 demonstrates this relationship.

Figure 3.1 Predicted Percentile Ranking of Student Proficiency in Schools, by the Overall Level of Teacher Leadership

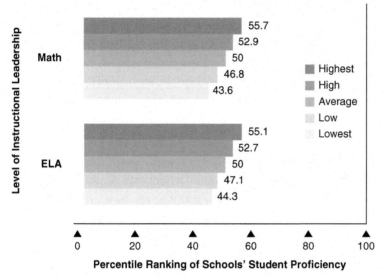

Source: Ingersoll, R., Sirinides, P., & Dougherty, P. (2017). School Leadership, Teachers' Roles in School Decisionmaking, and Student Achievement. Working Paper (#WP 2017-2). Consortium for Policy Research in Education, University of Pennsylvania. Used with permission.

Even with guidance about what teacher leadership looks like and the significant evidence that empowering teachers increases efficacy and positively influences student achievement, educational institutions are lacking clarity and coherence around how a school or district might cultivate teacher leadership practices. As with the examples referenced in this book, context is critical. The National Network of State Teachers of the Year website indicates, "The purpose of the [TLMS: Teacher Leader Model Standards] . . . is to stimulate dialogue among stakeholders of the teaching profession about what constitutes the knowledge, skills, and competencies that teachers need to assume leadership in their schools, districts, and the profession (TLEC, 2017)." There is no single roadmap to guide teacher leadership efforts, and yet, we can look to case studies of successful implementation to guide our thinking and develop practices that empower teachers and thereby positively improve student achievement.

VIGNETTE 3.1

Linden Instructional Leadership Teams

The boardroom was crowded with teachers from several schools receiving their "Future Ready" certification from the state of New Jersey. Once acknowledgments were completed an hour into the meeting, Interim Superintendent Denise Cleary announced that it was time for the annual presentation of district-wide assessment data. Denise stated to the teachers, "It's late and you all have to teach tomorrow. You live and breathe these data every day, so it's up to you if you want to stay for the presentation. I'm confident you all know this information inside and out!" Although they had not originally realized this was part of the agenda, every teacher attending the meeting decided to stay.

District Data and Assessment Supervisor Derek Kondratowicz stood and began to share the 2019 assessment results with the school board. The room was quiet as he referred to previous years' performance and compared the results with the current school year. A quiet buzz began to build as everyone in the room saw that their results showed a significant improvement in a number of grade levels. Derek then focused the group's attention on Grade 5. This was a significant group of students because it represented those most directly aligned to the district efforts

Figure 3.2 Linden Public Schools PARCC Grade-Level Outcomes

	Not Yet Meeting (Level 1)	Partially Meeting (Level 2)	Approaching Expectations (Level 3)	Meeting Expectations (Level 4)	Exceeding Expectation's (Level 5)	District % >= Level 4	NJ % >= Level 4
LINDEN PUBLIC SCHOOLS SPRING 2019 PARCC GRADE-LEVEL OUTCOMES ENGLISH LANGUAGE ARTS/LITERACY							
Grade 3	14.5%	22.7%	23.8%	36.1%	3%	39.1%	50.2%
Grade 4	8.1%	18.7%	28.8%	36.4%	8.1%	44.5%	57.4%
Grade 5	6.4%	10%	21.9%	52.6%	9.1%	61.7%	57.9%
Grade 6	12%	23.8%	33%	26.6%	4.6%	31.2%	56.1%
Grade 7	11.1%	15.7%	26.6%	35.6%	10.9%	46.5%	62.8%
Grade 8	15.4%	16.8%	22.4%	30.2%	15.2%	45.4%	62.9%
Grade 9	15.1%	4.9%	26.7%	33.8%	9.6%	43.4%	55.9%
Grade 10	17.6%	13%	21.2%	32.1%	16.1%	48.2%	58.9%

Note: **Numbers may not sum to 100% due to rounding.**
Source: Linden Public Schools. Used with permission.

at creating instructional leadership teams in each school. Those efforts began in 2016 when the fifth-grade students were second graders. After three intensive years of a district focus to empower teachers, the fifth grade in Linden outperformed the state in English Language Arts—for the first time in the history of the school district (Figure 3.2).

The room erupted in cheers and applause from the entire community: the public, school board members, administrators, and educators. It was a cause for celebration. While they still have room to grow, the entire community shared a common goal and—more importantly—the belief that they have the collective power to achieve that goal.

What Is an Instructional Leadership Team?

In 2016, a group of teachers and administrators in Linden, New Jersey, got together to discuss a problem that was puzzling them. They observed their teachers across all 11 schools working extremely hard. If they were working so hard, why wasn't student achievement improving? Why were the students not reaping the benefits of all that effort?

After much discussion, the group decided to bring together more stakeholders in the interests of diversifying their thinking: if the small group was having trouble determining root causes, perhaps they needed more perspective. Once the larger and more representative group convened, they began to realize that the hard work of educators was not having the impact they hoped because it was not cohesive or concerted—everyone was putting in a lot of effort, but not necessarily with a common goal or vision.

So what to do? The group realized that there were some things that had to change and so they revisited the recommendations outlined in the district's five-year strategic plan. The plan, created through the work of community stakeholders, first considered and revised the mission and vision of the Linden Public Schools. The group firmly embraced the need to rebrand the perception of Linden so that diversity—previously viewed as a challenge—would be seen as a strength. They reconsidered their notion of who should be involved in the work, noting the need to involve the community at all levels. Most importantly, they realized that their focus on curriculum and instruction had to be supported by data. While they had always examined data, they hadn't really drawn significant conclusions that would help inform practice.

Change is hard, and sustainable systemic improvement is even tougher. Led by a dedicated core group of teachers and administrators, Linden's change efforts really began when they embraced a distributed leadership approach. The heart of their initiative was the creation of instructional leadership teams (ILTs) composed of teachers, coaches, and administrators from each school in the district. Linden's theory of action was that leadership teams would foster a more systemic approach to their work. As identified by the Deeper Learning Research Series, policies to address issues of inequity must include "systemic learning that enables educators, schools, and agencies to learn from one another" (Noguera, Darling-Hammond, & Friedlaender, 2015, p. 16).

The ILT approach was shared with building-level administrators who were asked to create a team of teacher leaders interested in school improvement efforts. It was an unpaid position—and administrators were not sure what to expect when the invitation was first offered. To their amazement, approximately 100 teachers/instructional coaches expressed an interest and joined the ILT initiative. Coordinating coach Reina Irizarry-Clark shared, "We worked them hard that first year. And at the end, I thought—these people are not going to come back next year. But they did! And it keeps going!"

In the first year, the ILTs used a New Jersey process of school improvement based on the Connected Action Roadmap (CAR). As a processing tool, CAR helps to connect standards, student learning, assessment, professional learning, and school culture. The Linden team realized that in order to achieve coherence, everything they do must connect to the larger vision and serve to advance it. With almost half the students in Linden Public Schools speaking a language other than English at home (National Center for Education Statistics [NCES], 2019), there was a clear need to address instruction with an equity lens—were learners receiving intentionally designed supports?

Linden's first efforts served to build strong leadership teams by asking this essential question: whose responsibility is it to drive improvement? After much discussion, the ILTs came to consensus that the district culture needed to shift from one in which teachers viewed the district as accountable for making change, to one where everyone in the community owns the process. As one teacher put it, "Each student at [our school] is *everyone's* student and *everyone* has buy-in to their academic successes."

> Change is hard, and sustainable systemic improvement is even tougher.

Overcoming Challenges

Early on, the ILTs faced a number of challenges. While the district had spent time reviewing data, they hadn't always generated a plan of action to use the information revealed through data analysis. This is where they started. Their first meeting held after school consisted of a deep dive into data analysis that introduced teachers to strategies for making sense of and then using information from their assessments. They continued by offering webinars in the evening on various professional learning topics, encouraging teachers from across the district to return to work well after the school day was over. Teachers attended a summer series of sessions that offered a variety of learning topics. Superintendent Dr. Danny Robertozzi noted, "It's a tribute to the dedication of our teachers that they get together on their own time to make sure our students are getting the best education possible. These workshops strengthen the concept of teamwork and camaraderie among our staff and pay great dividends in the classroom."

Engaging meaningfully with data was not the only challenge. The existence of the ILTs became divisive at first. There was a perception that some teachers had been elevated to a more "preferred" status. To address this, the ILT members patiently worked with their colleagues to reinforce that their role was to provide logistical support and share essential learning and strategies. By emphasizing that this is "all of our work," they began to address misconceptions that had initially surfaced. In their school-based sharing sessions, ILT members honored the diversity of perspectives and expertise in the room, creating safe, judgment-free spaces for conversations that gave educators permission to raise concerns, brainstorm strategies, and build trust in each other. Most importantly, the ILTs kept the focus on student work and used a gradual release model that allowed colleagues to step into leadership roles whenever possible.

Evidence of Success

While standardized assessments are not the ultimate benchmark of success, the district has seen a steady rise in performance on both the state-mandated assessment and local assessments such as the Measures of Academic Progress (MAP), Developmental Reading Assessment (DRA) scores, and locally developed common assessments. Equally important is the noticeable shift in staff perceptions, from a focus on individual accountability to collective impact.

After the fourth year of ILT implementation, another significant sign of success appeared—quite unexpectedly. As Denise Cleary explains, "You have to understand . . . for years, Linden has had to combat this image of a struggling district with low test scores, a transient population, and a significant number of students in need of remediation. Really not a great public perception about the schools. And this year, one of our elementary schools—that has always underperformed until recently—was just granted national blue ribbon status. That is a true turnaround."

A significant shift in the ILT work came after years of creating data walls that were displayed in a secure location in each school. Teachers would create cards for each student with critical assessment data and display these on presentation boards so that the students could be sorted by performance level and the data could inform intervention practices. As the ILTs continued the practice, grumblings about the time-wasting nature of creating the boards were heard across the district. The need to allocate school space for secure display became a burden. One teacher noted, "We're spending way too much time cutting and pasting instead of focusing on how to help the kids!" The teachers recognized the value of the data walls once they were completed—it was creating and maintaining the walls that felt onerous.

As a result, the district developed a digital tool that allowed teachers to look at student performance on a range of assessments. Because they developed the tool themselves, they were able to include all of the features the district educators felt were important. Would you like to see how your previous students are currently performing? Check. Would you like to see how your class is performing compared to their grade-level peers? Check. Would you like to sort your class by performance levels on a particular assessment so that you can group them for intervention? Check.

One of the really interesting things to note is that all of the functionality that was built into the data tool meant that *all* teacher information was now open and available for the entire district to see. The decision to make all data open and transparent was highly intentional. As Derek put it, "If we are truly united in our efforts to support all of our students, we can't be hiding behind privacy walls." In many schools and districts, this would be a significant cultural issue; many data display tools are quite limited in that teachers can only access their own student information.

"If we are truly united in our efforts to support all of our students, we can't be hiding behind privacy walls." –Derek Kondratowicz

Derek noted that the openness of the tool would only have been possible after three steady years of ILT work in which the culture shifted from a focus on *my* students and *my* performance to *our* students and *our* impact. It took years of steady emphasis on data, *not* as a reflection on teacher performance but on how much educators must embrace those data to inform their practice. As a result, there was not a single complaint about the transparency of the new digital tool—only heartfelt thank-yous for the ability to more efficiently access critical student information.

This new way of thinking represents a critical shift toward equity, as Linden educators shifted their thinking to focus on what individual students might need. As the Race Matters Institute (2014) stated, "The route to achieving equity will not be accomplished through treating everyone equally. It will be achieved by treating everyone equitably, or justly according to their circumstances."

How Does Empowering Teachers Develop Collective Efficacy?

In this chapter, we focus our attention on one of the specific conditions that fosters collective efficacy: empowered teachers (Figure 3.3). By year two of the Linden initiative, Assistant Superintendent Denise Cleary noted, "We realized that what we had been doing was building

Figure 3.3   A Model for Leading Collective Teacher Efficacy: Empowered Teachers

"The route to achieving equity will not be accomplished through treating everyone equally. It will be achieved by treating everyone equitably, or justly according to their circumstances" (Race Matters Institute, 2014).

collective efficacy!" After realizing they had unintentionally tapped into the elements that contribute to fostering collective efficacy, the teams decided to increase their focus specifically on efforts that empower teachers. This recognition that efficacy beliefs were strongly in place early in the implementation process was key to strategizing how to continue moving the work forward (Figure 3.4). When strong efficacy beliefs are made visible and used as a springboard for sustaining the efforts over time, teachers move from being inquisitive to becoming proactive. They shift from adapting their current practices to innovating in the interest of meeting student needs.

> When strong efficacy beliefs are made visible and used as a springboard for sustaining the efforts over time, teachers move from being inquisitive to becoming proactive. They shift from adapting their current practices to innovating in the interest of meeting student needs.

Figure 3.4   Receptiveness to Change During Stages of Implementation Matrix

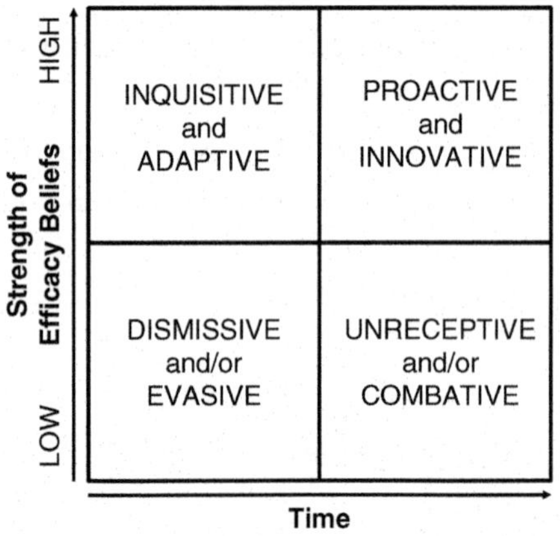

Teacher leadership was enhanced by incorporating more intentional participatory leadership practices into the work. The teams recognized that anyone in the district can play a leadership role both formally and informally. Teachers were empowered to make decisions about what the data were revealing and what they might do to address what was being revealed. They made decisions about how to relay the information to their colleagues in their home school and encouraged colleagues to make instructional decisions based on their new understanding.

> Past research has identified the strong and positive relationship between teacher influence (Goddard, 2002; Ross et al., 2004), teacher leadership (Derrington & Angelle, 2013), and collective teacher efficacy. Goddard (2002) concluded that where teachers had the opportunity to influence important, instructionally relevant school decisions, they also tended to have stronger beliefs in the combined ability of the faculty to positively impact student achievement.

Interdependent work was intentionally designed so that educators felt comfortable sharing their approaches, receiving feedback from colleagues, and co-creating new knowledge and understandings. Linden began incorporating Learning Walks into their ILT efforts during year two. This fostered a culture of trust and collaboration to such an extent that Linden is now embracing Opening Classroom Doors, a form of both internal and external rounds work in which teams of educators visit classrooms, collect student-focused data,

> In contrast to more hierarchical or autocratic leadership styles, the participatory leadership approach embraces high levels of transparency and collaborative decision-making. Participatory opportunities within an organization yield tangible benefits such as increased productivity and decreased absenteeism as well as intangible benefits such as increased employee motivation and job satisfaction.

aggregate and analyze the information, and offer improvement suggestions to their hosts. It is an extremely powerful way of bringing the learning community together. One high school teacher remarked, "The first thing I thought after visiting other classrooms is, 'I am in awe of the work done at the elementary level.' I had no idea! It was really powerful, and all of us immediately saw the value of participating in the visits." Consequently, teachers began to reach out to the administration asking, "Please keep me in mind for the next time we schedule Opening Classroom Doors." From the beginning, teachers realized the power of vicarious experiences as they visited classrooms both in their own home school and in schools across the district. Readers will learn more about the Opening Classroom Doors approach in Chapter 4.

The new Linden mission, developed as part of the five-year strategic plan, became the driving force for district change. Their decision to use the mission as the central focus for all of the ILT work meant that their efforts revolved around common understandings and

> A Learning Walk is typically a brief opportunity for small educator teams to visit classrooms during instruction. They vary in terms of size, focus, and intent but usually involve some form of individual or team feedback.

created cohesiveness in their efforts. At a more granular level, the ILTs have consistently embraced a "Here's what! So what? Now what?" reflection and analysis when reviewing data. Each team completes the following stems after reviewing external or internally collected data:

- *Here's what:* The data reveal . . .
- *So what:* This is important to student learning because . . .
- *Now what:* As educators, our next step is . . .

The use of these stems continually refocuses the teams on common understandings and common goals so that they continue to bring coherence to their work. This coherence represents the social persuasion occurring as the mission developed, the teams were established, and the work spread across the district.

Linden educators realized they could harness the leadership teams' social persuasion by explicitly sharing common goals and increasing their understanding of each other's contexts and efforts. This was achieved when designing the structure of the ILTs so that they would bring educators from all campuses together on a regular basis to focus on a common purpose. These intentional meetings allow for shared understanding of student needs as well as the instructional thinking required to address equity concerns across schools. As one teacher commented, "Being on the ILT has given me opportunities to collaborate with colleagues and experts. I leave each meeting feeling excited and eager to utilize what I learned and to turnkey that information. The energy and passion in each session is contagious." The emotion evident in this quote illustrates the importance of affective states in building collective efficacy.

Data and Assessment Supervisor Derek Kondratowicz began as a teacher on the high school ILT and then moved into an administrative role. He describes the process, now in its fourth year: "We feel like this is the norm for us now . . . it's a completely different district. To think that four years ago, we didn't even know what DOK [depth of knowledge] meant. Personally, I've learned more in the past three years than ever before in my career: being part of the team, bonding over the data, the ability to talk with each other and trust that we're all working toward the same goals. It's a complete transformation." In this reflection, Derek sums up the power of mastery and vicarious experiences, social persuasion, and affective states.

A Leadership Mindset

When we consider how best to empower teachers, we have to recognize the factors that lead to empowerment. Daniel Pink (2009) wrote about what motivates us in his book *Drive*, describing the three main ingredients: autonomy, mastery, and purpose. And when we look at the nature of many high-stakes teacher evaluation programs, they often run contrary to those three big ideas. In a high-stakes evaluation system, the concern is often more about attaining a proficient score rather than embracing a personalized journey of professional growth. Jim Popham (2013) wrote that the best people to identify growth opportunities are teachers themselves. "But if the teacher is interacting with an evaluator whose mission, even partially, may be to excise that teacher from the teacher's job, do you really think most teachers are going to candidly identify their own perceived shortcomings for such an evaluator? Not a chance!"

> A leadership mindset describes the dispositions of one who
>
> • holds aspirational goals for themselves and their team,
> • believes in and actively cultivates leadership potential in others,
> • creates a psychologically safe environment that fosters transparency and collaboration, and
> • regularly offers and seeks feedback that leads to continuous team learning.

(p. 18). Ever since Race to the Top legislation was passed in 2009, the hyperfocus on individual teacher evaluation has led to inconsistent and prescriptive plans for teachers, a lack of consensus about best practices, and ultimately, actual "gaming of the system." These outcomes are disempowering to teachers and in complete contradiction to the three drivers of intrinsic motivation: autonomy, mastery, and purpose.

To foster teacher empowerment, leaders must shift their mindset about teachers as the *target* of improvement efforts and recognize that teachers— particularly teams of teachers—are the *drivers* of school improvement. Once that awareness is solidly in place, leaders can begin to cultivate environments that foster strong adult

> Mastery is not only a driver of intrinsic motivation, it is also the number one source of efficacy. Mastery experiences generate an influential source of efficacy because repeated success raises future expectations for success (Bandura, 1998).

learning and collaboration. As Peter Senge et al. (2012) wrote in *Schools That Learn*, "'Rank and yank' systems had rarely, if ever, worked effectively in business. In truth, there rarely are that many poor performers in a professional environment; the problem is that there are so many hurdles that make it difficult to perform well. Rather than creating a hostile climate for low performers, the way to raise teacher quality is to create an environment more conducive to continual learning and development for the teachers" (p. 57).

Those with a leadership mindset consider the lenses of autonomy, mastery, and purpose to create a culture of empowerment:

- How much say do teachers have in the decision-making that happens in the school and district? Teachers are often granted *autonomy* in terms of their individual classes, but how frequently are they given an opportunity to come together as a learning community and make decisions that affect the overall operations and climate of the school or district?

- When do teachers have an opportunity to share aspects of their practice with their colleagues, representing their *mastery* in a particular area of instruction or pedagogy? By creating opportunities for teachers to learn from and teach others, they are provided with mastery moments that build their self-efficacy.

- How do teachers share in the creation of the school culture? That participation creates meaning in their work and builds a sense of *purpose*. It's not enough to rely on teachers inherently believing that their work has meaning; they must be actively engaged in the shared vision that drives purpose.

Leaders can use these questions to become reflective of their own practices; this is an essential first step when introducing the structures that foster a culture of empowerment for all members of the learning community.

How Can We Empower Teachers in Our School or District?

Creating the conditions that empower teachers is a complex endeavor and greatly depends on understanding local context and a group's readiness for change. One way of thinking about the systems in which we work is to use the lens of the Chaordic Path. "Chaord" is a portmanteau of *chaos* and *order*. *Order* is the preferred state of most systems and organizations because order equates with predictability: we know how to work together, we can look to past practice to guide us, and work requires less effort because we can more easily coordinate what we do.

Chaordic Path is a term used by the Art of Hosting community as part of their set of open source tools for building the communication skills critical to meaningful collaboration.

Chaos is often perceived as a negative, but it is in the messiness of chaos that creativity emerges and flourishes. Consider times when events transpired so that our past practices weren't as helpful; the chaotic nature of a situation where we can't rely on what we've done before forces us to think more innovatively about how to address challenges.

The Chaordic Path is a model based on a recognition of this natural tension between order and chaos. When a system is working in an orderly and predictable way, all is well. However, in the uncertain and complex times we are currently living in, the status quo is not always acceptable. In order for our education systems to avoid devolving in chaotic environments, we need to become innovative and flexible to address challenges. By thinking about how to harness the power of the area between chaos and order—the Chaordic Path—we can intentionally create an environment that fosters innovation (Figure 3.5).

Consider the Linden ILT example using the Chaordic Path lens: the district began with a highly structured approach. They determined that each school would create a representative team of instructional leaders who would receive information and professional learning relevant to student success. They then took a more chaotic approach to the next step by acknowledging that the manner in which teams would bring that information and training back to their buildings had to resonate in the local context. Some teams shared information during formal sessions for the entire faculty. Some teams worked in professional learning communities or grade-level team meetings. Some used

Figure 3.5　The Chaordic Path

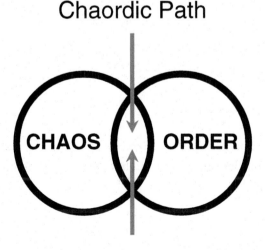

Chaordic Path

the face-to-face method of reaching out to colleagues during more individual or small group sessions. By using a *Chaordic* approach, each team had the freedom to design their way through local contextual challenges.

Follow the Chaordic Stepping Stones

One tool that we often use with groups who want to embrace the Chaordic Path is a set of guiding questions termed the Chaordic Stepping Stones. Using conversational methodologies, we coach groups to plan around each of the stepping stones in order to balance order and chaos. The stepping stones are a way of creating some structure (order) while allowing for creative thinking (chaos). It is a delicate balance because too much structure might inhibit or stifle creativity and too little structure might lead to a lack of cohesion and ineffective efforts.

The Chaordic Stepping Stones vary depending on the group and local contextual considerations, but essentially follow nine steps:

PART ONE: Inviting

1. Define the NEED, the compelling reason to do this work. Creating a NEED statement clarifies the reason for undertaking an initiative.

2. Determine the PURPOSE, the organizing statement that describes the efforts that will address the NEED.

3. Develop PRINCIPLES, which are a set of agreements about how we work together—this is very important when work becomes increasingly challenging.

4. Invite the PEOPLE by determining who should be involved at different levels of the initiative.

PART TWO: Implementing

5. Envision the OUTPUTS to outline the concrete outcomes of working together on this initiative. What might success look like?

6. Develop the ARCHITECTURE that supports the work: resources and necessary influence to get the job done.

PART THREE: Structuring

7. Develop the CONCEPT or the actual shape of the work accomplished together. For example, to cross a body of water, one concept might be a bridge. Another might be a tunnel.

8. Name the LIMITING BELIEFS that might stand in the way of success or derail the initiative.

9. Identify the STRUCTURE of the work by defining the tasks and timelines that will guide efforts.

Step 9 is typically where many teams choose to begin their work, jumping quickly to the action-planning phase. Without carefully considering the need to be addressed and the purpose of the work, identifying the right people, and clarifying how they will work together, many efforts wither during implementation. As a result, schools and districts often add a new initiative without carefully considering the reasons why previous efforts might not have been successful. This often leads to "initiative fatigue," described by Reeves (2010):

> Education leaders have three essential resources: time, money, and emotional energy. Time is fixed. Financial resources are typically fixed and, in the present economy, diminishing. Emotional energy is variable but has limits that are exhausted quickly by school leaders who ignore the reality that even the most dedicated employee can be resilient but will refuse to be an eternal Bobo doll, rising from each punch to endure another blow. The Law of Initiative Fatigue states that when the number of initiatives increases while time, resources, and emotional energy are constant, then each new initiative—no matter how well conceived or well intentioned—will receive fewer minutes, dollars, and ounces of emotional energy than its predecessors. (p. 27)

When considering an initiative designed to empower teachers in a school or district, it is essential to plan carefully for the right amount of structure and freedom (order and chaos), consider local contextual factors, and avoid initiative fatigue with a thoughtful and intentional approach.

The Linden story clearly illustrates the delicate balance of order—the concept of Instructional Leadership Teams—and chaos—team freedom to adjust their work to the needs of each local school. When considering how to empower teachers, a critical element to building collective efficacy, finding the right balance is essential.

Conclusion

Empowering teachers is an important precondition that can be considered as both formal educator roles and informal leadership opportunities. As we learned from Linden Public Schools, the nature of teacher leadership must be considered as an evolving idea with ever-increasing opportunities for their professional growth. Empowered teachers are not content to narrowly focus on instructing their assigned students, but aspire to contribute systemically to the entire learning community. Linden's model of Instructional Leadership Teams is one method of empowering teachers to consider their collective responsibility to all students in the district, impacting the culture of learning for all stakeholders and enhancing student achievement outcomes.

The nature of teacher leadership must be considered as an evolving idea with ever-increasing opportunities for their professional growth.

Cohesive Teacher Knowledge 4

Improvement and Change Do Not Follow a Linear Trajectory

In the interest of fostering cohesive teacher knowledge, many schools and districts talk about teacher collaboration, engage in professional development sessions, create professional learning communities (PLCs) and professional learning teams (PLTs), or provide department meeting time. The goal of a professional team should be to focus on instructional improvement and student needs. Unfortunately, team meetings are often diverted by the day-to-day demands of running classrooms and schools: Who is collecting field trip permission slips? How should we organize the end-of-year assembly? Who knows how to fill out the classroom repair requisitions? Even more productive, allotted meeting times often result in teachers dividing and conquering in order to accomplish pragmatic tasks that move their immediate work forward: grading assessments, completing forms, or discussing plans and logistics for school activities. In truth, simply providing meeting time does not mean that teachers are building cohesive knowledge about each other's practice.

> Cohesive teacher knowledge is defined as the degree to which teachers are aware of the teaching practices of others and their agreement in regard to what constitutes effective assessment and instructional practices.

Figure 4.1   Perception Versus Reality

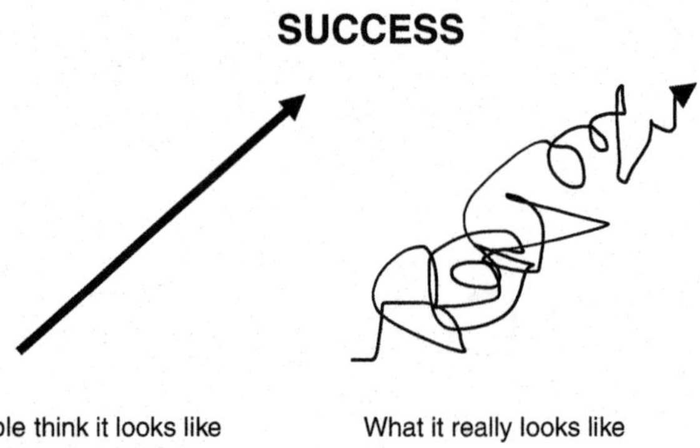

SUCCESS

What people think it looks like   What it really looks like

In reality, there is no one simple solution (Figure 4.1). To build cohesive teacher knowledge requires intentionally designed structures that embed the key elements of collaboration: a complex challenge worthy of our work together; both individual and group accountability; and the time, space, and resources to accomplish common goals. How these elements are designed depends greatly on local contextual factors, and the designs require frequent assessment for impact and redesigning as we learn more. This work is not simple.

> "Increasing self or collective efficacy in the absence of learning can lead to overconfidence" (Lindsley, Brass, & Thomas, 1995, p. 651).

> Complex work requires the persistence, perseverance, and endurance that is afforded through collective efficacy.

Many of the case studies we have presented represent years of committed effort and overcoming many bumps in the road. The truth is, success does not happen in a linear and orderly fashion. Learning is required in order to succeed. Katz and Dack (2013) defined learning as a permanent change in thinking and behavior. Learning—the kind that produces success—requires a willingness to innovate, acknowledgment of mishaps and mistakes, and adjustments to practice based on new understandings. At times, it may feel as if efforts are not producing any improvement at all. Complex work requires the persistence, perseverance, and endurance that is afforded through collective efficacy, especially when teams do not see immediate results. Complex work requires a willingness to embrace messiness and mistakes because the process will not be smooth. And complex work

> "If people experience only easy success, they come to expect quick results and are easily discouraged by failure. A resilient sense of efficacy requires experience in overcoming obstacles through perseverant effort. By sticking it through tough times people emerge more able and stronger from adversity" (Bandura, 1998, p. 54).

requires hope and optimism because it is impossible to strive for a more positive future without vision and a belief in what is possible to achieve. In the end, complex work is the most rewarding, often because of the challenges that must be overcome in order for it to have an impact.

VIGNETTE 4.1

The Power of Group Reflection

The 20 principals sitting around the table expressed emotions ranging from frustration to outright anger. Stef couldn't blame them—she had taken part in a San Antonio school district initiative during the first month of school that involved a series of classroom walkthroughs lasting three to four minutes, with the intention of rating teachers' instructional ability on a four-point scale. It was hastily constructed, was not well designed, and resulted in very upset teachers and building administrators. The walkthroughs proved to be disruptive and yielded stacks of rather useless data.

So here it is, a month later, and the charge was to undo what had been done. Whether the original plan had been well meaning or not, there were reparations to be made now. The group engaged in a circle check-in to give each principal an opportunity to express their frustrations and concerns. Stef listened and took notes. After each person had an opportunity to share, she apologized for what had happened. While Stef hadn't designed the walkthrough initiative, it was clear that someone needed to say they were sorry.

The group engaged in another round of circle practice, this time asking the team of administrators to reflect on what they believed might rebuild trust, reimagine the original intent of the walkthroughs, and consider what would be a meaningful step forward for the cohort of 20 schools. One by one, the principals offered their thinking and gradually, some patterns emerged.

"Well, we *do* need to know what's happening in the classrooms—there is too much about each teacher's instructional practice that's hidden."

"How should we get back into classrooms so that teachers don't feel threatened? How can we do it differently than those walkthroughs?"

One of the principals mentioned that the district had provided all of them with a copy of *Instructional Rounds in Education* (City et al., 2009), "but we never did anything with it." The cohort superintendent suggested that a more thoughtful approach to classroom observation, using the instructional rounds model as guidance, might be a way to regain trust. With that idea, the group turned its energy from frustrated venting to co-creating a new approach to their work as a professional network.

What Is Opening Classroom Doors?

Educators visiting teachers' classrooms to observe instructional practice and then discuss their learning is not a new concept. In their seminal book *Instructional Rounds in Education*, City et al. (2009) described the need for observing in classrooms as a way to build a common understanding of instruction and generate agreements about what it *should* look like. The authors describe the rounds process as "an explicit practice that is designed to bring discussions of instruction directly into the process of school improvement . . . a set of protocols and processes for observing, analyzing, discussing, and understanding instruction that can be used to improve student learning at scale" (p. 3).

Instructional rounds originated as a practice adapted from the field of medicine. Physicians have long used medical rounds as a way of improving both their understanding and practice by engaging groups of physicians to visit patients, observe and collect evidence, then thoroughly discuss possible treatments. In its original conception, instructional rounds were intended to be a formal opportunity for educational leaders to gather as a network, visit classrooms to gather evidence of instruction, and then focus on solving emerging problems of teaching and learning. Of particular concern in San Antonio was the issue of instruction for their population of students considered at risk (73.3%, according to the *Texas Tribune* in 2019)—was the learning environment providing them the support they needed to achieve grade-level expectations?

In the San Antonio vignette above, the administrative team was interested in embracing instructional rounds as a way to get a more meaningful and accurate understanding of current practices. In response to their needs, the leadership team conducted training sessions for the principal network that would be observing and collecting data. An instructional rounds specialist was brought in and the group established themselves as a network to practice objective, nonjudgmental data collection. One principal volunteered her school to be the first to host an instructional rounds session, and the staff engaged in deep conversations about their *Problem of Practice* and *Learning Look-Fors.*

In the instructional rounds processes, the Problem of Practice is a specific area of focus that the school determines to be an issue or an area in which the educators feel they need specific feedback. In the first attempt at conducting instructional rounds, the host school chose the following Problem of Practice: Students struggle with articulating a clearly defined learning target, connecting it to a learning goal, and interacting at high cognitive levels with that goal and the aligned learning task. Based on that Problem of Practice, the host school requested that the network gather data around Look-Fors related to the identified problem:

- What is the level of teacher and student questions?
- What is the level of student participation in activities?
- What opportunities are there for students to make connections with each other and participate in the activities?
- What supports are in place for students?
- What type of feedback are students receiving?
- How well can students articulate the learning objective, its relevance, and the success criteria?

Despite the training and preparation, the first instructional rounds session revealed unforeseen logistical complications (what do you do when several team members have emergencies at their building and can't attend?); unexpected procedural issues (how do you reconcile and mesh data when network members followed different collection methods, despite the training everyone had received?); and general messiness (how do you eat lunch and keep the work going within the confines of a small classroom at the host school?). Most importantly, the network did not realize until after visiting classrooms and reviewing their data that they didn't truly have a clear and common understanding of the Look-Fors. When asked, "How well can students articulate the learning objective?" the participants had very different conceptions of what a successful articulation might sound like. In light of the challenges, one would think that the first session would be the last. However, the network universally and resoundingly agreed that it had been an intensely valuable day of learning. As one principal put it, "I *finally* got to talk about teaching and learning instead of building management issues!"

However, the leadership team knew some adjustments needed to be made. The first few changes were logistical: taking into consideration that emergency absences will happen, the team established a deep bank of alternative participants. The host schools took care to create work spaces that would accommodate the teams' work on large charts and extensive use of sticky notes. District leaders took over the job of supplying materials and food for the teams so that host schools weren't scrambling to provide resources.

One of the most important adjustments was around building goal consensus, based on the realization that for the ultimate analysis of the collected data to have value, the teams needed clear agreements about the intention of the Look-Fors. Ultimately, a radical readjustment was made to differentiate between the Observing Team (the groups that would visit classrooms together to collect data) and the Look-Fors Team (individual members of the Observing Team responsible for observing the same Look-Fors). This learning came after critical reflections from the first few rounds sessions, resulting in a clear understanding that those collecting the same Look-Fors data need to have the same lens and be very clear on their procedures and intentions before observing in classrooms.

These adjustments resulted in the next few instructional rounds sessions operating more smoothly. More importantly, the network reported that their learning was increasing. They weren't expending as much energy worrying about conducting the rounds and were able to devote more time and thought to considering the best ways to collect their data and discuss optimal student learning behaviors. As the principal network increased their understanding, they brought their learnings back to their schools. As a result, host schools became more adept at defining and focusing their Problems of Practice and Look-Fors, which, in turn, helped improve the work of the visiting observers.

The most important "aha!" moment came when some "substitutes" participated because of inevitable emergencies. A few assistant principals and instructional coaches were called in to replace principals who were unable to leave their buildings. The leadership team was initially concerned that the experience would be frustrating because these folks hadn't been trained in the instructional rounds process. To address this concern, "newbies" were carefully placed on teams with seasoned veterans who could shepherd them through the data collection, aggregation, and analysis pieces.

As a result, the original principal network members reported that their learning increased dramatically because their role shifted to one of coaching. While the new participants said they were originally intimidated about being thrown into the process with little preparation, they quickly acclimated to the coaching model that naturally developed. As a result, they expressed that it was "an amazing day of professional learning."

At the end of the first year of practicing these modified instructional rounds, the original principal team met for a reflective debrief. Among their findings were the following:

- The original instructional rounds model was a great foundation; however, it was critical to make modifications that addressed local contextual needs.

- Establishing data teams that met to plan and strategize around individual Look-Fors proved to be valuable and the network wanted more explicit direction for that work.

- The host schools appreciated the opportunity to consider meaningful Problems of Practice and Look-Fors and found the data collected by the instructional rounds team to be useful. However, the deepest learning occurred for the observers. Therefore, the team expressed a strong desire to create opportunities that would include more participants, especially classroom teachers.

This last finding was a significant shift away from the original intent of instructional rounds—the creation of a consistent network of learners. The idea that new participants would join with little to no training also flew in the face of conventional rounds. However, City (2011) acknowledged that the largest benefit of instructional rounds participation was in doing the observation—not in being observed. The benefit stems from viewing student learning without a "fixing" lens, and instead looking systemically at instructional practices in a descriptive—rather than evaluative—manner. Therefore, the adjustments still addressed the spirit of ongoing instructional rounds work. This was an important recognition that efficacy beliefs were still low at a fairly early stage in the implementation; this required thoughtful consideration about how to modify the original plan so as to avoid potential dismissiveness or evasion (Figure 4.2).

Figure 4.2   Receptiveness to Change During Stages of Implementation Matrix

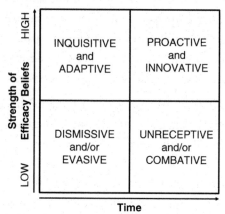

Based on the group's feedback, the team readjusted the original instructional rounds process to include new observers during each subsequent session, intentionally including classroom teachers. They continued to use a coaching model to support the work by partnering new participants with seasoned instructional rounds veterans, both in their Observing Team (those visiting classes together) and with their Look-Fors Team (those collecting data around the same instructional focus). The Look-Fors Teams were reconceptualized as *Data Teams*, following consistent practices for analysis by

1. converting their qualitative information into a quantitative response that answers the question raised in the Problem of Practice,

2. categorizing the quantitative responses to demonstrate trends during the observation period,

3. providing objective interpretations and wonderings suggested by the data, and

4. hypothesizing what the interpretations imply for student learning.

With a more clearly defined Problem of Practice and more focused Look-Fors, the teams were able to be more targeted in their data collection and analysis efforts. As a result, the analysis left behind for the host school provided more tangible action items for educators to consider. These transformations of the original instructional rounds process resulted in increased learning for the participants and an increase in targeted improvement efforts by the educators in the host schools.

As the work progressed in San Antonio during the second year, Stef began using these new approaches in other locations: Grand Rapids Public Schools, Houston Independent School District, and Linden Public Schools among others. In some districts, external instructional rounds (sending observers from one school to another) weren't logistically possible, so the process was adjusted to conduct classroom visits internally. In these other locations, groups reported that the language around *Problem of Practice* implied a negative presupposition that caused some anxiety to those opening their classrooms for observations. This resulted in shifting the language to explore a *Point of Inquiry*, noting that what makes the staff curious about student learning might not necessarily be negative or a problem. This emphasis on inquiry proved a nuanced but important modification and resulted in a noticeable increase in teacher engagement when they discussed their curiosities and wonderings about student learning without naming them as *problems*.

The result was a new process, built on the philosophy and intentions of instructional rounds, modified for local contextual needs, and enhanced with new approaches from data teams and coaching traditions. The process was called Opening Classroom Doors and has resulted in various iterations in schools and districts around the world, with positive results for both educators and students.

> "Constant inquiry and continuous individual and collective development are essential to professional success" (Hargreaves & Fullan, 2012, p. 22).

> "High-quality peer interaction among professionals doesn't evolve from nowhere or emerge by chance." It depends on expectations and frameworks of learning that are "challenging and open enough for teachers to innovate and inquire into their practice together (to have something significant to meet about)" (Hargreaves & Fullan, 2012, p. 87).

Evidence of Success

The original San Antonio cohort saw increased student achievement on their state assessments. After three years of Opening Classroom Doors efforts, students showed enough growth that several schools on the "Improvement Required" list were removed. One of the schools improved to such an extent that the principal is now working at the district level, specializing in how to turn around failing schools. As an example, a steady increase in Briscoe Elementary's state

Figure 4.3   Briscoe Elementary School's State Assessment Data

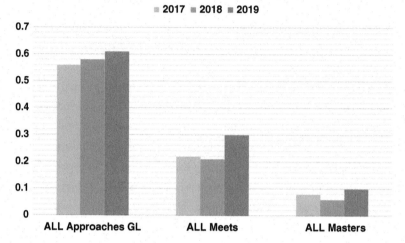

Briscoe Elementary STARR

■ 2017 ■ 2018 ■ 2019

assessment data (State of Texas Assessment of Academic Readiness) can be seen in Figure 4.3. Despite significant external influences (91.4% of the students are economically disadvantaged, 32.9% are English language learners, and 77% are identified as "at risk"), the staff's work toward collective efficacy is having a consistent impact on increasing student achievement and addressing achievement gap issues.

One of the most powerful examples of the impact of vicarious experiences comes from the day Briscoe Elementary hosted its first external visitors for Opening Classroom Doors. After several teams of teachers spent time collecting data in a particular classroom, there was a hushed and somewhat agitated conversation in a corner of the debrief room. Stef moved to head off a potential problem and asked if there was an issue that needed to be addressed. After a long pause, one of the teachers expressed the group's concern, "because we know this isn't supposed to be judgmental or evaluative and I feel like we're 'telling on' a colleague . . . but there is a whole class of gifted students that we visited in fourth grade. That's against district policy—gifted students aren't supposed to be homogeneously grouped—but we're not sure if we should be saying anything." In the interests of transparency, we brought the principal, D'Les Gonzales Herron, over to respond to the concern. The teachers shared that—clearly—an entire class of students was drawn from the school's gifted population. "What makes you say that?" asked D'Les. "Well, they were working on a really high-level activity where they had to develop menus based on dietary requirements and budget. They were working in groups and they called themselves 'the scholars.' They said they were lucky because they were in the 'master class.'" An enormous smile spread across D'Les's face and she gleefully told the concerned group, "Can I tell you that not one of the children in that class scored proficient on the state assessment last year? But I'm pretty sure they will this year!" The group of teachers was stunned. After some more conversation, one of the teachers turned to Stef and shakily admitted, "I think we have been completely underestimating our students."

This realization is an incredibly important outcome of the cohesive teacher knowledge built in San Antonio schools. A growing body of research suggests that lowered expectations in schools and districts play an enormous role in unequal access to rigorous academic experiences and highly qualified teachers for English language learners and minority students (TNTP, 2018). Addressing the inequity of access is not just an operational issue; educators must have their eyes opened to the assumptions and biases they didn't realize existed.

> Addressing the inequity of access is not just an operational issue; educators must have their eyes opened to the assumptions and biases they didn't realize existed.

An indicator of success for any educational initiative is whether or not it resulted in a permanent change in thinking and practice. Teachers who participated in the Opening Classroom Doors efforts in San Antonio found such value in observing their peers that they expressed an eagerness for more eye-opening experiences, even when funding was no longer available.

> "Models are a source of aspiration, competencies, and motivation. Seeing people similar to oneself succeed by perseverant effort raises observers' beliefs in their own abilities" (Bandura, 1998, p. 54).

D'Les Gonzales Herron, while still principal at Briscoe Elementary, included teachers on classroom visits to create "snapshots" of data that were shared in a weekly memo. These snapshots included data similar to the Look-Fors data collected during the Opening Classroom Doors initiative, with reflection questions for teachers to consider their impact on the data collected. The memo also showcased engaged student learning in action in an effort to continue to increase teacher knowledge of each other's work. D'Les commented that the foundation was there because teachers had gotten comfortable with opening their doors and visiting their colleagues' classrooms to such an extent "that the culture was established so that we could keep the work going." During the initial stages of the implementation, educators adapted their practices as their efficacy beliefs strengthened. As the structure of Opening Classroom Doors changed over time, they became proactive in maintaining the

Figure 4.4   Receptiveness to Change During Stages of Implementation Matrix

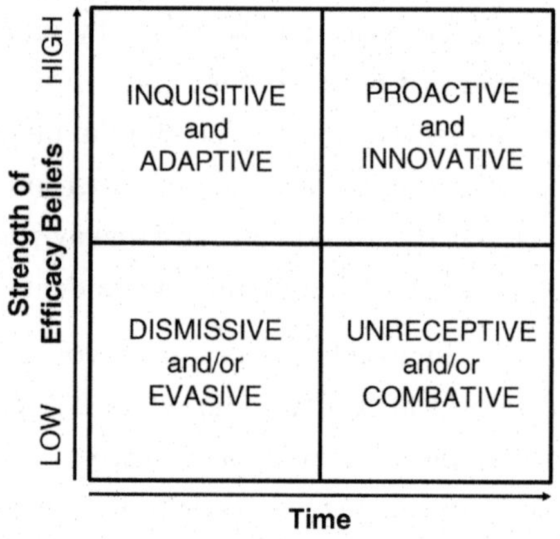

"open door" spirit of the initiative, finding new ways to continue sharing their knowledge of each other's work in the interest of supporting their students (Figure 4.4).

We have now been steadily working in other large districts using Opening Classroom Doors as a means to increase efficacy through vicarious experiences. Linden Public Schools (readers read about Linden Schools in Chapter 3) is now in its second year of intentional classroom visits, both internal (visitors from within the school) and external (teams of visitors from other schools in the district). While still early in the implementation, reflective data from teachers indicate a higher level of awareness regarding the intersection of student learning and their own practice. For example,

- "Being able to bounce ideas off colleagues and listening to others' perspectives and impressions was invaluable. I was especially impressed at the way we were all able to work together productively with a common goal."

- "The collaboration with my peers and seeing the work done in other classrooms really motivated me to reflect on my own teaching."

- "You are not alone in the struggles within your own classroom. You can see a piece of your own practice in every room you visit and see how to make your practice better."

These comments reflect how cohesive teacher knowledge—combined with goal consensus and empowered teachers—creates an ongoing experience that embeds reflective practices into the day-to-day work of educators. These experiences create the optimal conditions for tapping into sources of efficacy, enhancing both individual and collective teacher efficacy.

How Does Cohesive Teacher Knowledge Develop Collective Efficacy?

In this chapter, we have focused on cohesive teacher knowledge as one of the important conditions that foster collective teacher efficacy (Figure 4.5). The structure of Opening Classroom Doors touches on multiple elements that have been shown to develop collective teacher efficacy. When teachers have an opportunity to visit classrooms and observe students while not being responsible for their instruction, they have a unique, vicarious experience opportunity. Rarely are classroom teachers encouraged to put themselves in the shoes of their students. During the observations, they ask themselves questions such as, What is the optimal learning behavior given the student's

Figure 4.5   A Model for Leading Collective Efficacy: Cohesive Teacher Knowledge

instructional goal? How well does the student understand the demands of the work and have the agency to move forward in their understanding? As a Master Teacher from San Antonio put it, "As I participated [in Opening Classroom Doors] it made me reflect upon myself as an educator. I analyzed my classroom to determine if I, as a leader, delivered rigorous lessons."

When engaging in Opening Classroom Doors, whether as the seasoned veteran coach or the new participant, the entire team has an opportunity for a shared mastery experience. By careful structuring and facilitation, team members are able—in the course of one school day—to visit classrooms during instruction, gather important and meaningful data, aggregate those data as part of a larger team, and conduct an analysis of what the data might indicate for next steps. Teachers and administrators alike report the pride they feel after a day of intensive work and note how it is almost "magical" how it all comes together. An elementary principal in Grand Rapids stated, "It was eye opening how quickly we could create a plan of action for the campus."

Opening Classroom Doors is a prime example of interdependent work. The hosting school staff works to reach consensus around their Point of Inquiry and Look-Fors. The Observing Teams must work together to collect data and then aggregate and analyze them for sharing back to the host school (or their colleagues). As teachers participate more and more in doing the observing (rather than being observed), they develop the skills that make a systemic difference in the lives of students beyond the four walls of their classroom. As a principal from Houston put it, "I think that more teachers should be involved in the process . . . [they] can be more reflective, mindful, and intentional in their classroom practice and the ways in which they impact students, families, as well as fellow colleagues of the campus, district, and community at large."

> Research demonstrates that the relationship between collective efficacy and performance is maximized when there is positive interdependence amongst team members (Gully, Incalcaterra, Joshi, & Beaubein, 2002).

Opening Classroom Doors relies on educator interdependence; it is impossible to conduct the observation, data gathering, analysis, and forward planning without working together as a team and achieving goal consensus. While there are many efforts to increase teacher interdependent work in schools, creating structures that increase the need for teachers to be interdependent encourages individual teachers to think and act as a team. Opening Classroom Doors provides clear expectations about individual roles during the effort, and it sets a common purpose for the work. The experience builds teachers' knowledge about each other's work in a collaborative, learning-oriented environment, and this leads to co-construction of new knowledge. The resulting empowered teachers lead to increased collective efficacy.

How Can We Use Opening Classroom Doors to Build Cohesive Teacher Knowledge in Our School or District?

A defining characteristic of Opening Classroom Doors is that it is customized to meet local contextual needs. The design should carefully consider the existing culture within the school or district. That being said, there are some general structures that provide the starting point for any system that wants to embrace this powerful approach to developing collective efficacy. Consider two different approaches:

- **External instructional visits**—teams of educators from various schools meet at a single host building for a structured day of visiting classrooms to see student learning in action.

- **Internal school instructional visits**—teams of educators from within a single school engage in a structured day of visiting classrooms to see student learning in action.

One of the most important aspects of Opening Classroom Doors is that it is not about individual teacher practice or evaluation; it is about the student learning experience and our collective responsibility to students.

Consider the essential characteristics that create the structure of Opening Classroom Doors:

- **Point of Inquiry** (POI)—an unresolved question or curiosity around student learning that focuses on one element of practice and involves shared inquiry.

- **Learning Look-Fors**—targeted student learning practices for which we can collect data when visiting a classroom during instruction.

- **Data Collection**—focused information gathered according to a process designed by the Look-Fors Team to collect nonjudgmental and nonevaluative data about the student learning experience.

- **Data Team Analysis and Sharing**—team aggregation and analysis of the data, followed by discussion of how to learn from the results in order to improve the learning experience for students.

Develop the Point of Inquiry

The *Point of Inquiry* must be developed as a common curiosity about student learning that is shared by all educators. There are a number of characteristics that define a strong Point of Inquiry:

- It should be clear and directly related to instruction.

- It must be observable by watching students in the learning environment.

- It must be actionable (under our control).

- It should be high leverage.

This final characteristic is important because most schools have more than one curiosity or dilemma about student learning. When that is the case, we should choose to focus our attention on the item we believe will have the greatest impact on our students' learning. Some examples of Points of Inquiry from our Opening Classroom Doors work are as follows:

- How authentically engaged are our students in their learning?

- Is learning collaborative? What structures are in place for students to help each other learn?

- How are our students demonstrating their willingness to take educational risks?

- What is the level of academic challenge experienced by our students?

- What supports our students to persevere in the face of challenge?

- How do students know the quality of their work?

- What responsibility are students taking for their own learning?

Construct the Look-Fors

Once the Point of Inquiry question is developed by the educators through a consensus-building process, we ask them to describe the learning belief behind their curiosity. For example, one school's Point of Inquiry was, "What responsibility are students taking for their own learning?" and this was founded on a belief that students must be authentically engaged and have some internal motivation in order to achieve academic success. Once this belief was clarified, the next step was for educators to describe what success would look and sound like. If students were to take responsibility for their own learning, we would expect students to

- articulate (in their own words) the learning intentions and their importance/relevance;
- articulate (in their own words) the success criteria;
- describe self-reliant strategies for getting "unstuck" when work becomes challenging;
- be working collaboratively on activities that
  o represent a high level of challenge,
  o require interdependence, and
  o require some level of individual accountability;
- be holding high-level (as measured by Webb's Depth of Knowledge) conversations with each other; and
- be respectfully debating with each other as they work.

This vision of student success provides clear guidance for the type of data to be collected during classroom observations. The statements are converted into data collection Look-Fors to guide the visiting teams as they observe students during instruction.

Address Opening Classroom Doors Logistics

Once the Point of Inquiry and Look-Fors are developed, the next challenge for schools is to handle the logistics for Opening Classroom Doors. Whether the observations are external (visitors from outside the school) or internal (visitors from within the school), careful consideration to the schedule is a must for a smooth experience. The goal is to create a structure that allows the participants to focus on the task of observing, collecting data, and analyzing rather than worrying about fluctuations in the schedule, timing, or materials.

The first job is to determine the teams: who will be observing in classrooms, and who will be opening their doors to allow visitors time to gather data? For many of the schools and districts we've worked with, asking for volunteers to open their doors is a wise first step so that educators do not feel this is an initiative that is forced on them. While internal visits may instinctively seem like a logical first effort in Opening Classroom Doors, it turns out that many teachers are actually more comfortable with external visitors, rather than starting with their colleagues from down the hall! In one district in particular, we intentionally began their journey with external visits and only began internal visits when educators were clear that this was a nonevaluative and collaborative effort.

The number of visiting teams varies depending on the size of the school. We have found that the optimal size for teams is three or four data collectors. We assign each member of the team one of the Look-Fors determined by the host school so that they have a focused lens when collecting their data during the visit. Therefore, teams of three can accommodate three Look-Fors and teams of four can accommodate four Look-Fors. Any more than four team members is an overwhelming number of adults to circulate through a classroom, so we recommend keeping teams small.

Once the teams have been determined, the next challenge is to create the schedule of visits. We highly recommend that teams visit classrooms in 20-minute intervals, with teams rotating through classrooms so that each period of instruction is observed for a total of 40 minutes. This provides a longer observation period in terms of data collection but minimizes the time teachers spend in one classroom, thus reducing bias and increasing objectivity. See Appendix F for sample schedules and agendas.

We recommend that the observation times be structured to allow for data collection to occur during optimal instruction time for students. This means that developing the schedule is a logistical challenge because we want to avoid times when students are out of the classroom, on breaks such as recess or lunch, or during major transitions. Once this work is accomplished, the agenda for a day of Opening Classroom Doors is shared with all educators: both those opening their doors and those visiting to collect data.

There is no aspect of this work that should be kept secret. In the interest of transparency, we have found that it is wise to provide frequent reminders of the Point of Inquiry, the Look-Fors, and the guidelines for visiting classrooms:

- Focus on student learning (not teacher instruction).

- Collect objective, nonjudgmental data (no analysis during visits).

- Leave a thank-you note for the teacher who opened their door.

- Minimize lesson disruption.

- Hold team discussions *only* in the debrief space.

It is essential to be vigilant about the nonevaluative nature of Opening Classroom Doors. While there are other opportunities for teachers to receive individual feedback—during formal observations by supervisors or peer observations by colleagues—Opening Classroom Doors is intentionally targeting our collective responsibility to students and therefore must focus on the collective student experience in a school. By taking care to remind the groups of the co-constructed Point of Inquiry and Look-Fors as well as the visitation guidelines, we support the creation of trusting environments where teachers feel a strong sense of belonging and motivation to engage in joint work.

With Opening Classroom Doors, we can clearly see a structure that creates cohesion amongst teachers, both in establishing common Points of Inquiry and then making decisions based on the data collected during classroom visits. How else can leaders support building cohesive teacher knowledge? As a brand-new teacher, Stef was lucky enough to be mentored by a masterful principal who regularly covered lessons so that teachers could visit each other's classrooms and then debrief during their grade-level meeting times. Before welcoming external visitors, Linden High School's leadership team introduced the "Pineapple Project," creating a schedule where teachers might volunteer to open

"Some of the most powerful, underutilized strategies in all of education involve the deliberate use of teamwork—enabling teachers to learn from each other within and across schools—and building cultures and networks of communication, learning, trust, and collaboration around the team as well. If you want to accelerate learning in any endeavor, you concentrate on the group" (Hargreaves & Fullan, 2012, p. 89).

their classrooms for colleagues to visit during their planning periods. Stef worked with a school where the educators were nervous about collegial visits and so they first experimented with "ghost walks," where they spent time as a team analyzing the learning environment, absent of students. Traditional faculty and department meetings can be shifted from a managerial focus to a learning session centered on instruction that allows teachers to develop knowledge of each other's teaching.

Building cohesive teacher knowledge takes time and requires that teachers not only gain awareness and knowledge about each other's work but also develop new understandings and build agreement regarding what constitutes effective assessment and instructional practices. When working with teams, Jenni has found protocols useful in supporting work with leaders to elicit the level of analysis needed to build such agreements. Protocols assist teams in safely exploring ideas through the examination and analysis of student work and/or artifacts of educator practice. The purpose of a protocol is to help teams move beyond merely knowing about what goes on in each other's classrooms to developing shared understandings of students' learning and their own instructional practices. We go into greater detail about protocols in the next chapter when discussing the enabling condition of embedded reflective practices.

The point of these examples is that Opening Classroom Doors is a philosophical idea, not just a professional learning design. We can open classrooms in many different ways, and embracing this philosophy is strengthened with the guidance and logistical support of a willing and supportive leader.

> We can open classrooms in many different ways, and embracing this philosophy is strengthened with the guidance and logistical support of a willing and supportive leader.

Conclusion

The path to improvement does not follow a smooth, upward trajectory. As we saw with the San Antonio vignette, there are often bumps in the road. In pursuit of building cohesive teacher knowledge, we have to be willing to learn from mistakes by engaging groups in deep and meaningful reflection and being willing to make adjustments to our thinking. When groups are able to develop clear understandings around the complexities of teaching and learning, there is a higher likelihood that reflective practices will become regularly embedded in an ongoing effort to improve instruction. One such method of creating cohesive teacher knowledge is by Opening Classroom Doors, both literally and figuratively.

Embedded Reflective Practices 5

Perceptions Are Critical to Confronting Inequity

As noted throughout this book, teachers' theories about students' socioeconomic status, race, and/or ethnicity affect the content and skills teachers choose to teach, their beliefs about students' ability to learn, as well as their beliefs about what they can do to increase student performance (Evans, 2009). In order to address the challenges of inequity in education, teachers must perceive themselves to be both individually and collectively capable of delivering effective instruction to underperforming and/or disadvantaged students in ways that will result in students' better performance and increased academic achievement. The more salient teachers' perceptions of the obstacles posed by students' socioeconomic status, race, and/or ethnicity, the lower their expectations and goals. Lower expectations result in teachers assigning low-level tasks to students and the lowering of students' own expectations about themselves. A teacher's diminished sense of efficacy results in less effort and a lack of receptiveness to integrating new approaches in practice.

In order to address the challenges of inequity in education, teachers must perceive themselves to be both individually and collectively capable of delivering effective instruction to underperforming and/or disadvantaged students in ways that will result in students' better performance and increased academic achievement.

VIGNETTE 5.1

Teachers' Receptiveness to Change

Jenni worked with a team of English teachers in a small, rural high school over the course of a few years. One year, they were engaged in a collaborative teacher inquiry that focused on improving students' ability to make inferences. Collaborative inquiry is a four-stage process where teams identify a common student learning need, create a plan for addressing the student learning need, implement the plan, and evaluate their results. During their PLCs, the English teachers shared texts, graphic organizers, and strategies they were utilizing in their classrooms. They also examined student work and tracked student progress over the course of the school year.

Jeff (pseudonym) was a veteran teacher and new to the school. He seemed particularly concerned about the students in a class he taught immediately after lunch. The class was mostly boys, and Jeff described them as disengaged and unmotivated. It was an "applied"-level course, which meant that upon graduation, students enrolled in the applied pathway are workplace bound rather than university bound (which is the pathway for students enrolled in "academic" courses). There was a very large gap in academic achievement between students in applied classes and academic classes, as reported on the standardized literacy tests at this high school. While 88 percent of students in academic classes were proficient, only 46 percent of students in the applied stream met proficiency in reading and writing.

Teams from school districts across the province of Ontario have engaged in collaborative teacher inquiry as a professional learning design. Two very targeted and ongoing initiatives are the Listening Stone Projects (promoting Indigenous education) and the Many Roots, Many Voices Projects (focused on improving progress and achievement of English language learners). Teams of educators and other stakeholders who have been involved in collaborative inquiry as an embedded reflective practice have been successful in increasing student achievement and strengthening collective efficacy.

Bruce and Flynn (2013) found that teachers engaging in a collaborative inquiry over a three-year period felt empowered to make instructional decisions together and that the learning design had a "positive impact on teacher beliefs about their abilities to help students learn" (p. 704).

Jeff indicated that he had tried many different strategies but didn't have much success with his afternoon class. He said the students were not capable of making inferences and that the *only way* to engage the boys was through reading materials that had to do with war and violence. The department head, Pete (pseudonym), agreed that the students were "a very weak group." As an invited and trusted member of the English team's PLC, Jenni facilitated the group in unpacking their assumptions that students could not infer and that students could only be engaged with violent content. Jenni then asked Jeff if he would be open to testing his theory that the boys were unable to infer.

Jeff invited Jenni into his afternoon class to teach. She selected three high-leverage strategies for teaching inference (chunking text, Know-Wonder T-chart so that students could draft and revise their thinking, and questioning "What made you think that?"). Jenni also selected a high-interest text (Joseph Boyden's "Walk to Morning"). During the lesson, students engaged, revised their thinking, made predictions and inferences, and defended their opinions with evidence

> "Holding low expectations of students contributes to gaps in learning and achievement primarily through the types of learning opportunities teachers provide students . . . [A]lthough studies have consistently demonstrated that constructivist approaches are effective with students who live in poverty, such pedagogy is least often used" (Budge & Parrett, 2018, p. 79).

and high-quality reasoning. Every single student contributed. Now as a side note, we want to be clear that it was the strategies that made the difference (not Jenni). Having a bunch of observers in the classroom may have had a minor influence on a couple of the students, but the large majority were engaged and learning because of the strategies—which any teacher can employ. At the end of the period, when the students filed out of the class, Jeff sat silently. Jenni held back her thoughts. Pete was the first to speak: "I feel ashamed for assuming that these kids couldn't infer. Every one of them had incredible insights and even Shane contributed to the discussion! I am going to use those strategies in my class." Jeff remained unconvinced, however. He shrugged it off as "just the novelty of having someone new teaching them."

For some teachers (like the department head, Pete, in Vignette 5.1), witnessing success being modeled under similar circumstances (the same group of boys who were "incapable" of inferring, in the same classroom, immediately following lunch) was enough for him to recognize and reveal his bias and change

> Rubie-Davis, Hattie, and Hamilton (2006) explored the impact of students' ethnicity on teachers' expectations and found that teachers' sustaining low-expectation effects were an explanation for Maori students' limited progress over the course of a year.

his beliefs. This is an example of a vicarious experience. It was a powerful vicarious experience because as a result of seeing someone else achieve positive outcomes (boys' engagement, participation, and ability to make inferences), Pete's sense of efficacy was strengthened. "If someone else can do it, in our school, with that afternoon class of boys, then I can do it too." Equally important, it raised Pete's expectations about what the students in that afternoon class were capable of doing.

"Observing one perform activities that meet with success does, indeed, produce greater behavioral improvements than witnessing the same performances modeled without any evident consequences" (Bandura, 1977, p. 197).

To see it modeled wasn't enough, however, for Jeff, the hosting classroom teacher, to shift his attributions of student success and/or failure to what was within his control. Nor was it enough to increase Jeff's expectations of his students. Shifting long-held fundamental beliefs takes time. "The broader social conditions in which teachers live and work, and the personal and professional elements of teachers' lives, experiences, beliefs and practices are integral to one another" (Day, Kington, Stobart, & Sammons, 2006, p. 601). There are often tensions between these, which can have an impact to a greater or lesser extent on teachers' self-efficacy and collective teacher efficacy. Shifting attributions, raising expectations, and increasing teachers' sense of individual and collective efficacy is complicated work, requiring embedded reflective practices that are sustained over time.

Shifting attributions, raising expectations, and increasing teachers' sense of individual and collective efficacy is complicated work, requiring embedded reflective practices that are sustained over time.

The strength of Jeff's efficacy beliefs was low, and as a result, Jeff avoided making changes to his practice as demonstrated in the lower-left

Figure 5.1   Receptiveness to Change During Stages of Implementation Matrix

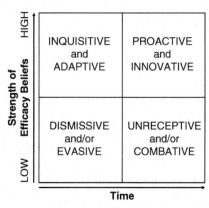

quadrant of the matrix (Figure 5.1). Jeff's lack of efficacy made him think that his efforts wouldn't amount to much and so he was dismissive about what was required to improve the learning of his students. The strength of Pete's efficacy was higher (top-left corner of the matrix), and as a result, he was more inquisitive about trying something new in his practice. He was more willing to experiment with different approaches in his classroom.

Aspects of Embedded Reflective Practices

When teams embed reflective practice into their regular routines, it involves thinking critically about their professional work with the intention of improving it. Important aspects of reflective practice include

- collaborative examination of student learning data (What is our area of greatest need?);

- identification of evidence-based approaches (What should work in theory?);

- repeated trial of evidence-based strategies in classrooms (How can we best leverage evidence-based approaches given our unique context and our unique students?); and

- re-examination of evidence (What is our collective impact? Are we making progress toward our goals?).

When teams of teachers engage in reflective practice, it helps to uncover beliefs and assumptions that drive actions and shift causal attributions for success and/or failure. In light of evidence of impact, the cause-and-effect relationship (teaching causes learning) becomes more evident and efficacy beliefs become enhanced.

Embedded Reflective Practices School-Wide

Garth Larson accepted the position as principal at Butte des Morts, a kindergarten through fifth-grade elementary school, in the summer of 2011. At that time, Garth explained, the school was "trending in the wrong direction on state assessments." The school's 2011–2012 accountability rating on the District's School Report Card (Figure 5.2) showed an overall score of 57.9 percent, which meant they were meeting few expectations. This was reflective of the downward trend the school had experienced for the previous seven or eight years. Garth explained that over that period of time, the school experienced a major

Figure 5.2 Butte des Morts 2011–2012 School Report Card

FINAL – PUBLIC REPORT – FOR PUBLIC RELEASE

WISCONSIN DEPARTMENT OF PUBLIC INSTRUCTION

Butte des Morts El | Menasha Joint
School Report Card | 2011-12 | Summary

Overall Accountability Score and Rating

57.9

Meets Few Expectations

Overall Accountability Ratings	Score
Significantly Exceeds Expectations	83-100
Exceeds Expectations	73-82.9
Meets Expectations	63-72.9
Meets Few Expectations	53-62.9
Fails to Meet Expectations	0-52.9

Priority Areas	School Score	Max Score	K-5 State	K-5 Max
Student Achievement	**50.0/100**		**66.4/100**	
Reading Achievement		20.0/50		28.5/50
Mathematics Achievement		30.0/50		37.9/50
Student Growth	**56.9/100**		**67.4/100**	
Reading Growth		27.9/50		34.2/50
Mathematics Growth		29.0/50		33.2/50
Closing Gaps	**41.3/100**		**65.7/100**	
Reading Achievement Gaps		21.5/50		32.6/50
Mathematics Achievement Gaps		19.8/50		33.1/50
Graduation Rate Gaps		NA/NA		NA/NA
On-Track and Postsecondary Readiness	**83.4/100**		**85.5/100**	
Graduation Rate (when available)		NA/NA		NA/NA
Attendance Rate (when graduation not available)		75.1/80		74.2/80
3rd Grade Reading Achievement		8.3/20		11.3/20
8th Grade Mathematics Achievement		NA/NA		NA/NA
ACT Participation and Performance		NA/NA		NA/NA

Student Engagement Indicators	Total Deductions: 0
Test Participation Lowest Group Rate (goal ≥95%)	Goal met: no deduction
Absenteeism Rate (goal <13%)	Goal met: no deduction
Dropout Rate (goal <6%)	Goal met: no deduction

School Information

Grades	KG-5
School Type	Elementary School
Enrollment	456
Race/Ethnicity	
American Indian or Alaska Native	2.4%
Asian or Pacific Islander	3.1%
Black not Hispanic	6.1%
Hispanic	17.5%
White not Hispanic	70.8%
Student Groups	
Students with Disabilities	15.4%
Economically Disadvantaged	68.6%
Limited English Proficient	13.2%

Wisconsin Student Assessment System Percent Proficient and Advanced

Includes Wisconsin Knowledge and Concepts Examination (WKCE) and Wisconsin Alternate Assessment for Students with Disabilities (WAA-SwD). WKCE college and career readiness benchmarks based on National Assessment of Educational Progress. **State proficiency rate is for all tested grades: 3-8 and 10**

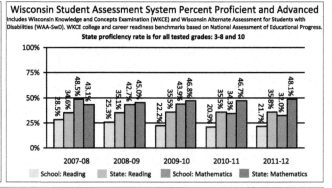

School: Reading State: Reading School: Mathematics State: Mathematics

Notes: Overall Accountability Score is an average of Priority Area Scores, minus Student Engagement Indicator deductions. The average is weighted differently for schools that cannot be measured with all priority area scores, to ensure that Overall Accountability Score can be compared fairly for all schools. Accountability Ratings do not apply to Priority Area Scores. Details can be found at http://dpi.wi.gov/oea/acct/accountability.html.

Wisconsin Department of Public Instruction | dpi.wi.gov
Report cards for different types of schools should not be directly compared.

Page **1**

Source: Reproduced with permission from the Wisconsin Department of Public Instruction, 125 South Webster Street, Madison, WI 53702; (800) 441-4563.

change in demographics. As industry became less prominent in the Fox Valley (located in Appleton, Wisconsin), home rental prices dropped to the lowest level in the surrounding area and government subsidies increased; 68.6 percent of the student population was identified as economically disadvantaged. "Under the previous leadership the staff did not have a chance to understand the shift in demographics. They now needed to teach students with very diverse experiences and learning gaps and needed support in doing so."

Upon Garth's arrival, he put together a leadership team with teacher representatives from kindergarten through fifth grade. Due to the downward shift in their accountability rating, efficacy beliefs were at an all-time low. Expectations for student success were low as well and excuse-making was at an all-time high. Garth knew he needed to help teachers experience success so that they would realize their collective capability to impact positive change. He began by engaging the leadership team in reflective practices and asking questions such as "What are our beliefs about the students we serve? What assumptions are driving those beliefs? And do our students feel valued, welcomed, respected?" Some of the staff had assumptions that students living in poverty were not capable of achieving to a high standard. Teachers believed that the way they experienced school was the same way they should deliver instruction. Since they experienced success in a traditional teaching environment as students, shouldn't everyone experience success the same way? The teachers were not yet equipped to implement district improvement efforts, such as Response to Intervention (RTI), because they lacked relationships with the students. Garth explained that he needed to "change the narrative" while making sure that teachers' voices helped to "shape the new narrative" he desired to create.

Garth worked with the team in identifying a new vision for the school—one that would spark optimism and hope for a different kind of future. Rather than saying

> "It's crucial for educators to keep in mind the many factors, some of them invisible, that play a role in students' classroom actions. Many nonminority or middle-class teachers cannot understand why children from poor backgrounds act the way they do at school. Teachers don't need to come from their students' cultures to be able to teach them, but empathy and cultural knowledge are essential" (Jensen, 2009, p. 11).

"the way we've experienced school is the way it should be," Garth helped the staff to understand students' lived experiences in order to better meet their needs. Garth encouraged teachers to gain as much knowledge about their students as they could through student interest inventories and discussions about students' likes and dislikes. Once teachers knew more about their students, they could integrate this knowledge into their daily lessons. Studies by researcher Lisa Delpit (2006) show that students really need to see connections between their lived experiences and learning. Once teachers knew more about their students, they could include this information and draw connections between activities within the home and school.

In the first year, Garth described a two-pronged approach: high expectations for students and relationship building. The leadership team created and widely shared a set of high expectations for students attending the school and focused on "building relationships to ensure that students, staff, and parents felt valued, welcomed, and respected." The following fall (2012–2013), the school realized a fairly significant increase (10 percentage points) in overall proficiency on their School Report Card (moving from 57.9% to 67.9%—meeting expectations). Garth leveraged this as an efficacy-enhancing opportunity. Once the faculty became aware of the 10-percentage-point increase, "they realized what they were doing *was* making a difference and that *we do have the ability* to have a positive impact on students." Garth continued to explain the significance of the results from the first year. "We were amongst the lowest rated elementary schools in the state. That [increase] was a significant improvement. It took us from one of the lowest rated schools and placed us in the middle. It helped in building collective teacher efficacy."

In the second year, Garth encouraged the teachers to examine evidence more regularly in order to determine collective impact. "We used internal measures of growth and progress along with anecdotal

Bernhardt (1998) identified four types of evidence that can be used for school improvement. *Demographic data* provide descriptive information about the students and community. Examples include enrollment, attendance, ethnicity, gender, and so on. *Student learning data* provide information about results and include standardized tests, everyday assessments, report card marks, credit accumulation, and the like. *Perceptual data* help teams understand what students, parents, and teachers think about the learning environment. Finally, *school process data* define what teachers are doing to get the results they are getting. Examples include standards, curriculum, instructional strategies, and gap-closing interventions, to name a few.

evidence." Garth used multiple sources of evidence to help teams realize that their collaborative efforts continued to produce desired results. He continued to gather information about students' experiences. "Do our students feel valued, welcomed, and respected?" (perceptual data). He began to note fewer disciplinary office referrals and increased attendance (demographic data). He also saw teachers trying new and different instructional strategies (school process data). Student achievement continued to increase (student learning data).

Garth also noted that by the end of the second year, as principal he "could now place less emphasis on the district's annual assessments and the state standardized tests." Teachers were more frequently using quick assessments, checking-for-understanding techniques, and regular checks for progress. Garth quoted his friend and colleague, Cale Birk: "You don't change data by looking at data. You change data by looking at practice." As the teachers critically examined their professional practices, they took action to improve them.

> "You don't change data by looking at data. You change data by looking at practice."
> –Cale Birk

They spent the next few years identifying and implementing evidence-based approaches. They regularly monitored progress toward goals. Five years after Garth arrived at the school, results from the 2016–2017 School Report Card (Figure 5.3) showed an overall score of 85.8 percent, which significantly exceeded expectations. More importantly, Garth noted, was the student growth score (82.2/100) and Closing Gaps score (95.3/100). The Closing Gaps priority area focuses on measuring how much districts and schools contributed toward closing statewide gaps in academic achievement and graduation rates.

Closing Gaps in the Wisconsin Accountability Report Card assesses progress over time among historically marginalized student groups in the state, for whom they see large and persistent achievement and graduation gaps. The measure compares the trajectories of achievement and graduation rates among different groups over time (Wisconsin Department of Public Instruction, 2019).

The resulting pride (positive affective states) felt by the teachers further boosted their collective efficacy. As the teachers' sense of collective efficacy grew stronger, they became more hopeful and confident in dealing with challenging circumstances, reframing circumstances in ways that made them appear more manageable. Bandura (1997) noted that when teams believe they can exercise control over situations, they don't conjure up adversity; instead, they tend to create positive representations about what's possible.

Figure 5.3   Butte des Morts 2016–2017 School Report Card

FINAL - PUBLIC REPORT - FOR PUBLIC RELEASE   November 21st, 2017

Butte des Morts Elementary
Menasha Joint | Public - All Students
School Report Card | 2016-17 | Summary

Overall Score

85.8

☆☆☆☆☆
Significantly Exceeds Expectations

Overall Accountability Ratings	Score
Significantly Exceeds Expectations	83-100 ★★★★★
Exceeds Expectations	73-82.9 ★★★★☆
Meets Expectations	63-72.9 ★★★☆☆
Meets Few Expectations	53-62.9 ★★☆☆☆
Fails to Meet Expectations	0-52.9 ★☆☆☆☆

Priority Areas	School Score	Max Score	K-5 State	K-5 Max
Student Achievement		**63.9/100**	**69.4/100**	
English Language Arts (ELA) Achievement		30.0/50	34.7/50	
Mathematics Achievement		34.0/50	34.7/50	
School Growth		**82.2/100**	**66.0/100**	
English Language Arts (ELA) Growth		46.3/50	33.0/50	
Mathematics Growth		35.9/50	33.0/50	
Closing Gaps		**95.3/100**	**64.4/100**	
English Language Arts (ELA) Achievement Gaps		45.3/50	33.6/50	
Mathematics Achievement Gaps		50.0/50	30.8/50	
Graduation Rate Gaps		NA/NA	NA/NA	
On-Track and Postsecondary Readiness		**87.3/100**	**89.2/100**	
Graduation Rate		NA/NA	NA/NA	
Attendance Rate		76.1/80	75.4/80	
3rd Grade English Language Arts (ELA) Achievement		11.2/20	13.8/20	
8th Grade Mathematics Achievement		NA/NA	NA/NA	

Student Engagement Indicators   **Total Deductions: 0**
Absenteeism Rate (goal <13%)   Goal met: no deduction
Dropout Rate (goal <6%)   Goal met: no deduction

School Information

Grades	K4-5
School Type	Elementary School
Enrollment	421
Percent Open Enrollment	4.0%
Race/Ethnicity	
American Indian or Alaskan Native	0.5%
Asian	1.2%
Black or African American	2.9%
Hispanic/Latino	13.3%
Native Hawaiian or Other Pacific Islander	0.0%
White	75.1%
Two or More Races	7.1%
Student Groups	
Students with Disabilities	20.0%
Economically Disadvantaged	65.3%
Limited English Proficient	10.0%

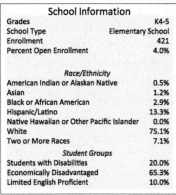
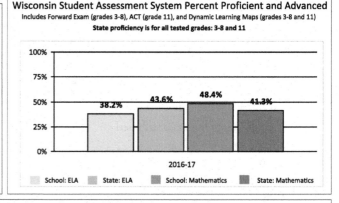

Wisconsin Student Assessment System Percent Proficient and Advanced
Includes Forward Exam (grades 3-8), ACT (grade 11), and Dynamic Learning Maps (grades 3-8 and 11)
State proficiency is for all tested grades: 3-8 and 11

(2016-17: School: ELA 38.2%, State: ELA 43.6%, School: Mathematics 48.4%, State: Mathematics 41.3%)

^Note: Outlier score fluctuation is noted by ^ when any school or district report card has a 10-point or greater change (up or down) in both Overall Score and Growth Score. This amount of change may or may not be reflective of actual school/district performance. DPI encourages review of other priority area scores in the detailed report card for a better understanding of school performance. Details: http://dpi.wi.gov/accountability/report-cards

Wisconsin Department of Public Instruction | dpi.wi.gov
Report cards for different types of schools or districts should not be directly compared.

Page 1

Source: Reproduced with permission from the Wisconsin Department of Public Instruction, 125 South Webster Street, Madison, WI 53702; (800) 441-4563.

How Do Embedded Reflective Practices Develop Collective Teacher Efficacy?

Embedded reflective practices encourage joint problem-solving and instructional experimentation. While determining solutions to problems, knowledge is generated by the team and that enhances individual teacher effectiveness. This, in turn, increases a teacher's perceptions of both individual and collective success, thus enhancing expectations for future success. As noted earlier, important aspects of embedded reflective practices include collaboratively figuring out how to make evidence-based practices work and determining collective impact. As teams engage in this type of interdependent work, they gain more intimate knowledge about each other's practice and build collective understandings about what constitutes sound pedagogy. As a result, teams become more cohesive and are more easily able to come to consensus on goals. Because they had the autonomy to make instructionally relevant decisions, a sense of teacher empowerment is also enhanced. In this respect, the enabling conditions represented in Figure 5.4 are interconnected and all contribute to collective efficacy further through Bandura's (1977) four sources of efficacy-shaping information.

Figure 5.4   A Model for Leading Collective Efficacy: Embedded Reflective Practices

Embedded reflective practices specifically tap into Bandura's (1977) sources in the following ways: First, embedded reflective practices help to create environments that legitimize help-seeking and peer support. When peers feel supported, they also feel less stress and anxiety. Therefore, the effects of negative emotions (i.e., negative affective states that diminish efficacy) are also likely to be reduced. Some teams may even achieve "collective flow" while engaging in this type of joint work. Traditionally, "flow" occurs at the individual level when individuals are completely focused and absorbed in an activity while experiencing total enjoyment (Csikszentmihalyi, 1990). Flow at the collective level can be understood as an optimal experience amongst members of a team characterized by emotional components such as enjoyment, satisfaction, confidence, and success. These positive affective states, which are generated when teams are able to meet difficult challenges, play a key role when influencing collective efficacy beliefs.

Salanova, Rodriguez-Sanchez, Schaufeli, and Cifre (2014) studied small workgroups and found that "a feeling of collective flow at the group level predicts how efficacious a group will feel over time" (p. 449). They also found a reciprocal relationship between collective efficacy and collective flow over time. They noted that findings provide empirical support that experiencing collective flow is due to the team's belief in the team's combined capability to overcome challenges in the future.

Second, embedded reflective practices influence how teachers interpret mastery and make it easier for teachers to recognize when they are successful. Understanding the influence of the collective contribution to teachers' individual successes is likely to be higher in schools where this type of interdependent work occurs. In this respect, individual teacher efficacy and collective teacher efficacy become reciprocal in nature. Third, embedded reflective practices provide opportunities for vicarious experiences as efficacy-shaping sources. By interacting with and gaining more intimate knowledge of each other's practices, teachers are enhancing their own effectiveness and individual efficacy. And finally, it was noted earlier that cohesion is built through embedded reflective practices. Ross et al. (2004) noted that "the more cohesive the faculty, the more likely teachers can be persuaded" (p. 167). Social persuasion is one of the sources of efficacy identified by Bandura (1977).

How Can We Support Embedded Reflective Practices in Our School or District?

Leaders can create environments where embedded reflective practices are part of the normative expectations of teachers' interdependent work and serve to close achievement gaps. We would like to re-emphasize that when using the term *leader* we are referring to both formal and informal leaders in schools. It's just as important for teacher leaders to consider which ideas in this book they can utilize to build efficacious teams as it is for formal leaders. Leaders can create environments where embedded reflective practices are part of the normative expectations by

- introducing into teachers' collaborations structures and protocols that help to facilitate reflection based on evidence;

- ensuring teams use disaggregated data and multiple measures as diagnostic and formative tools to help guide, inform, and assess improvement work;

- encouraging experimentation with evidence-based strategies; and

- providing efficacy-enhancing feedback to teams.

Each of these ideas is expanded upon further in the section that follows.

Introduce Structures and Protocols That Help to Facilitate Reflection Based on Evidence

In order to promote teams' embedded reflective practice, leaders can introduce structures and protocols. When using the term *structures*, we are referring to powerful learning designs—a kind of blueprint that identifies the steps or stages of a professional learning process or cycle. While professional learning structures help to focus teams' efforts and guide teams as they engage in this work, protocols provide tools to prompt reflective thinking and enhance psychological safety. Without structures and protocols, embedded reflective practices are unlikely to occur routinely at a team level. It is too often that teachers' collaborations are focused on issues that are unrelated to instructional improvement and addressing issues of inequity and instead concentrate on the organization of field trips, fundraisers, and so on. While intentions are good (we acknowledge the importance of field trips and fundraisers), collaboration that goes beyond event planning is essential to address issues of inequity.

> Some examples of structures that leaders in this book used to support embedded reflective practices included common formative assessments, Instructional Rounds in Education, Opening Classroom Doors, instructional coaching, and collaborative teacher inquiry.

Structures for Professional Learning

As noted earlier, important aspects of embedded reflective practices include collaborative examination of student learning data, identification of evidence-based approaches, repeated trial of evidence-based strategies in classrooms, and the re-examination of evidence to determine collective impact. Without a structure to help guide teachers through the stages of a professional learning process or cycle, the managerial demands of day-to-day instruction often sidetrack teams. When teams select a structure that is right for them and adhere to the stages, it helps minimize "activity traps." Katz, Earl, and Ben Jaafar (2009) used the term *activity trap* to describe the "convincing delusion" that is constructed based on the combination of good intentions and hard work. They describe activity traps as "a focus on the doings and not the outcomes" (p. 41) and noted that "if activity were a proxy for improvement things would be fine," but they also remind us that "levels of activity hold no direct promise for improvement" (p. 24). Structures like Opening Classroom Doors and collaborative teacher inquiry help to keep collaboration focused on outcomes and impact, which are importantly related to fostering collective efficacy.

> There are additional powerful professional learning structures beyond the ones mentioned in this book. We encourage readers to explore different approaches to determine what fits best with their team. Collaboratively determining the structures is an important part of the process.

> Easton (2009) described protocols for professional learning as "processes that help groups achieve deep understanding through dialogue" (p. 1). She suggested that the main reason educators would want to use protocols is that they do not want to be isolated in their own classrooms and "they know they can learn from others and, in turn, help others" (p. 11).

Protocols for Professional Learning

Protocols also help teams stay focused on outcomes and impact. A protocol is an agreed-upon guideline for a conversation. Protocols provide safety and guidelines for teams to engage in deeper conversations about professional practice based on sensitive topics like inequity. Some are very tightly prescriptive, detailing step-by-step directions, prompts, and timelines in which conversations are meant to occur. Some protocols are designed more loosely in that they are less prescriptive and provide less stringent guidelines. There is an abundance of protocols designed to help teams examine student work, identify and solve dilemmas of practice, analyze assignments and assessments, and consider evidence. There are also a number of equity protocols that are designed to help educators think more deeply about what diversity means, create space for making meaning on equity issues, and look at student and teacher work in order to understand it in relation to promoting equity.

Readers have been introduced to a few protocols through the stories of achievement in this book; this is by no means an exhaustive list of all of the possibilities. The most important aspect of protocols is that they provide structure and safety for teams to work together in meaningful and productive ways that embed reflective practices in their day-to-day work.

> One of our favorite sources for protocols is the National School Reform Faculty. Educators can find more than 200 protocols that have been designed to help teams "arrive at a specific desired outcome, efficiently and effectively," at https://nsrfharmony.org/protocols/.

It's been our experience that once protocols are embraced, meetings are transformed. No longer are teams diverted by the day-to-day demands of running classrooms and schools—they become focused on interdependent problem-solving. Well-designed protocols stimulate team reflection based on evidence of student outcomes, helping teams make the link between their professional practices and increases in students' performance. This information is an important efficacy-shaping source.

We have also, however, witnessed how teams can become protocol junkies: cherry-picking protocols for the sake of having a protocol. What we'd like to stress is the importance of selecting the right protocol for the desired outcome. Take the time to think about what it is your team is

> Birk and Larson (2019) designed PLC 2.0 in response to the challenges they identified with some existing PLCs. They noted that the goal of PLC 2.0 is to help educators reflect upon the work they are doing from "a lens of observable impact" (p. 21). The aim of PLC 2.0 is to "help schools and their collaborative teams to get clarity for themselves on one question regarding their PLC work: 'What is the observable impact of our collaborative efforts?'" (p. 21). The answer to this question becomes a powerful source of collective efficacy. Readers will recall that the most powerful source of collective efficacy is mastery experiences. Collective efficacy is strengthened when teams see the results of their combined efforts. As such, Birk and Larson (2019) have designed, tested, and revised a number of protocols that help teams engage in reflective practices regarding their impact.

trying to accomplish and then explore protocols for that purpose. Be true to the protocol. Katz and Dack (2013) noted that successful execution of some protocols requires that the group tolerate the discomfort that is an essential prerequisite for a permanent change in thinking and behavior. The temptation to make things more comfortable for a group might lead to protocols being revised and steps being skipped. When this happens, the opportunity to reshape beliefs is often lost. Finally, if the situation does not require a protocol, don't use one. Sometimes, all that is required is a regular conversation.

Ensure Teams Use Disaggregated Data and Multiple Measures as Diagnostic and Formative Tools

In order to promote embedded reflective practices, leaders can also help to ensure that teams use disaggregated data and multiple measures as a diagnostic and formative tool to help guide, inform, and assess improvement work. While school districts collect and maintain student data a bit differently, most have already undergone the process of storing and analyzing student-level data. Although there might be slight variations in the ways in which data are exchanged and reported within and across schools in a district, teachers' interpretations of data and the determination of actions to take as a result of data analysis *hinge upon leaders' effective selection and dissemination of information.* Evans (2009) noted that "leaders determine what information gets used or omitted, whether the information is accurate, who gets the information, and how the information is going to be used" (p. 83).

Disaggregated Data

Disaggregation of student data is when student population data are broken down into smaller groupings based on characteristics such as family income, English language proficiency, race and/or ethnicity, or gender. Teams need both aggregated data as well as disaggregated data that accurately describe smaller groups of students they serve. Detailed data about different subgroups of students can be a useful tool for improving outcomes because the progress and achievement of small groups of students might be otherwise indistinguishable if data are not broken down by subgroups. Having disaggregated information helps teams address inequity by identifying needs, planning appropriately, and allocating resources where they will have the most impact. Leaders can help teams use this information both as a diagnostic tool and for formative assessment. Disaggregated data can play a critical role in helping teams understand how effective they are in meeting the needs of *all* the students they serve.

An example of a leader's strategic use of disaggregated data was shared in Chapter 1 in the Maine Township story. Readers might recall that Ken Wallace shared data that demonstrated the district's changing demographics and data that highlighted that underserved students were not gaining access to advanced placement courses. He shared this information to help his team identify a need and to create an urgency to

> Teachers' interpretations of data and the determination of actions to take as a result of data analysis *hinge upon leaders' effective selection and dissemination of information.* Evans (2009) noted that "leaders determine what information gets used or omitted, whether the information is accurate, who gets the information, and how the information is going to be used" (p. 83).

address this inequity. Readers may also recall that in Chapter 3, Linden administrators chose to share student achievement data in a public board meeting, revealing the information to a cross-section of community stakeholders. This was a strategic sharing of data that served as a communal mastery experience, linking the impact of educators' collective efforts and positive student outcomes.

Disaggregated data must be handled carefully, as follows:

- Ensure sensitivity to the cultural issues in your school environment.

- Analyze and report data in ways that do not put subgroups at risk or perpetuate any existing stereotypes.

- Help teachers make sense of achievement gaps and frame data in ways that acknowledge collective responsibility.

- Keep privacy issues at the forefront when sharing information inside and outside of your school community.

Multiple Measures

Leaders can also encourage teams to consider multiple measures of evidence when engaging in embedded reflective practices. As noted earlier, Bernhardt (1998) identified the following four types of evidence that can be used for school improvement: demographic data, student learning data, perceptual data, and school process data. Like Garth Larson did at Butte des Morts Elementary School, leaders can help teams address the needs of subgroups by encouraging them to intersect multiple sources of evidence to inform their interdependent work. Leaders can ask questions such as, "Do our English language learners perceive the learning environment differently, and are their report card marks consistent with these perceptions?" (demographics by perceptions by student learning). Another example of a question that intersects multiple sources of evidence asks, "Are there differences in achievement scores for fifth-grade boys and girls who reported that they are engaged in school, compared to those who are not, by the sports and/or extracurricular programs in which they are enrolled?" (demographics by perceptions by school process by student learning). Effective efficacy builders do not wait for results from annual standardized tests to help teams see if they are making progress toward their goals. Like Garth, they use multiple sources of evidence from their daily work to determine cause-and-effect

Effective efficacy builders do not wait for results from annual standardized tests to help teams see if they are making progress toward their goals.

relationships. Teams examine evidence to determine if the strategies they used in their classrooms helped to advance students' understanding.

Encourage Experimentation With Evidence-Based Strategies

Another important aspect of embedded reflective practices involves teachers experimenting with different evidence-based strategies in their classrooms. Leaders can support this important aspect of embedded reflective practices by helping teachers engage with educational research in meaningful ways and supporting the sustained use of evidence-based strategies over time. These ideas are expanded upon in the section that follows.

Helping Teachers Engage With Educational Research

We have heard many educators argue that you can use research to prove just about anything. Many teachers we have spoken to dismiss research findings because they feel data are often misconstrued to promote the author's bias. Often, if one teacher locates a study, another teacher can locate a different study that has demonstrated contrary findings. Also, one study might claim that X is the most impactful way to increase student achievement while another study points to Y as more important. The truth is that there *is* significant variance in the impact reported on particular factors that influence student achievement and there are numerous reasons for this—which include the quality of the research study amongst other things. That is why it's important to look to meta-analyses when making decisions based on research.

A meta-analysis is a statistical procedure that combines the results from many individual studies on a particular topic. An effect size is calculated, which allows comparisons between and amongst variables. As noted earlier, the larger the effect size, the greater the magnitude of that particular variable on an outcome. A more precise estimation of the impact of that particular factor results from pooling the individual studies.

Many readers will be familiar with John Hattie's Visible Learning® meta-analysis. It's the largest synthesis of meta-analyses that examines factors that influence student achievement. Because meta-analyses provide a more precise estimation of the impact of particular variables than do individual research studies, leaders can look to the Visible Learning meta-analysis or other educational meta-analyses to help inform decisions. Educational meta-analyses add strength to the confidence of the reported outcomes (effects) of particular factors that influence student achievement. In other words, it's hard to dismiss research findings from meta-analyses because they provide a more precise picture of effects as predictors (or not) of student achievement.

Leaders can help teachers engage with educational research in meaningful ways. Building awareness is a starting point. Leaders can encourage teachers to access and carefully consider research findings when selecting strategies designed to address the learning needs of their students. Leaders can communicate information about the strength of the evidence for the influences in the Visible Learning database (e.g., student self-efficacy has an effect size of 0.71) to the teachers and help them in understanding what is meant in regard to various factors' potential to accelerate student learning or not.

Leaders can also select particular factors from meta-analyses and use them as opportunities to demonstrate the need to uncover the untold stories behind the effect sizes. Homework is a good example of an influence, from the Visible Learning database, that needs to be "unpacked" for teachers because it is affected by moderating variables. A moderator is a third variable that affects the strength of the relationship between the independent (e.g., homework) and dependent variable (student achievement). Corwin Visible Learning Plus (2019) demonstrated that homework has a higher effect size in high schools (0.64) than it does in primary grades (0.15). When the overall effect size of homework (0.28) is taken at face value it appears less significant than when it is disaggregated according to grade level. Leaders can help teachers understand this and engage them in learning more about the "stories" behind the influences they select and use in their practice.

Finally, leaders can also facilitate discussions about the relative merit of current and alternative approaches. As noted earlier, there are many protocols that are designed to engage teachers in reflective practices, and protocols help to separate "person" from "practice." Helping teachers and teams understand individual and collective impact is what is key; therefore, everyone benefits when reflecting on the relative merit of different approaches. Protocols help to keep discussions at a level of objectivity, which helps teachers take things less personally.

Supporting the Sustained Use of Strategies

Marzano (2012) added further explanation as to why the reported effect sizes of different instructional strategies vary from study to study. By analyzing video recordings of teachers using strategies, Marzano noticed different levels of implementation, ranging from beginning level (in which the teacher had little fluency with the strategy, which therefore had little effect on student learning) to an innovating level (in which the teacher is so familiar with the strategy that they are able to adapt it to meet specific student needs). The message here is that teachers need multiple opportunities to see strategies modeled and practice them in order to understand how to adapt them to meet the various learning needs of students. Too often, strategies are abandoned before teachers become fluent in their use. Leaders can support teachers by encouraging them to not abandon strategies too soon.

> Too often, strategies are abandoned before teachers become fluent in their use.

Provide Efficacy-Enhancing Feedback

We too often hear teams attribute reasons for lack of success in schools to factors that are outside of their influence. This might sound like, "We didn't expect much from those students—just look at the neighborhood in which this school is located" or "Those students didn't succeed because their parents are working two jobs and are never at home to supervise." We've also engaged in conversations with educators who attribute success to these very same factors. For example, when working with a team in a school that was located in a gated golf course community, Jenni pointed out the incredible results the school was able to maintain over the course of many years on a standardized Province test. The teachers and administrators explained it away: "Well, it's this neighborhood. These kids have doctors and lawyers for parents."

Socioeconomic status is an influence on student achievement that comes from the home and has an effect size of 0.52 (Hattie, 2019). Parental involvement is another factor that comes from the home and has an effect size of 0.45 (Hattie, 2019). We do not want to argue that these things do not matter. Clearly, they do. However, the research is also clear that collective teacher efficacy, which is an influence on student achievement that comes from the school, is over two times more predictive of student success than socioeconomic status. It is also more than three times more predictive of student success than parental involvement. Teams need to recognize

> Teams need to recognize that what they do really does matter.

that what they do really does matter over and above the educational contribution of students' homes and communities. Leaders need to help teams make the connection between their combined ability and effort and improvements in student results in order to foster collective teacher efficacy.

High-quality feedback from leaders can help teams make the connections between their professional choices and increases in student outcomes. This is a form of social persuasion (the third source of efficacy) and as Bandura (1977) noted, when quality feedback comes from a credible source, it can enhance the efficacy of a team. Credibility of the feedback provider boils down to two things: Can we trust this person? Can we believe what they are saying? The best ways leaders can build credibility is by being honest and transparent. Speak the truth and communicate reasons why decisions are made. Those receiving the feedback are more likely to internalize it when they trust you and believe you.

> Reeves (2010) argued that causes become irrelevant in environments where only effects matter. In many school improvement initiatives, educators are more interested in results (effects) than what caused those results (teachers' professional knowledge, combined efforts, teaching approaches, etc.). Leaders can build efficacy by helping teams make cause-and-effect relationships more explicit.

When considering how effective the feedback will be, not only does credibility come into play, but so does the type of feedback given. Three types of feedback can be used to shine a light on the cause-and-effect relationship between teaching and learning, and they are also important in relation to building efficacy. The three types of feedback are effort attributional feedback (feedback that links performance outcomes with effort), strategy attributional feedback (feedback that links performance outcomes with strategy use), and ability attributional feedback (feedback that links performance outcomes with ability). Examples of each are provided in Table 5.1.

In order to enhance efficacy, teams need to succeed at the very things they think they can't accomplish. Equally important, teams also need to attribute success to their combined efforts, strategies, and capabilities. By providing feedback that helps teams make the link between their effort, strategies, and capabilities and better performance, leaders can reshape the narrative in schools. The new narrative empowers the collective as the staff comes to realize that a different reality is possible. At this stage in reflective practice, when teams recognize that progress is being made toward a goal, they invest and put forth

> By providing feedback that helps teams make the link between their effort, strategies, and capability and better performance, leaders can reshape the narrative in schools. The new narrative empowers the collective as the staff comes to realize that a different reality is possible.

Table 5.1   Efficacy-Enhancing Feedback

Effort Attributional Feedback	Strategy Attributional Feedback	Ability Attributional Feedback
"This year our graduation rate is at an all-time high! I know it's a result of our combined efforts. All that additional time we spent supporting students has really made a difference, and more students will graduate because of it."	"I've observed a few classroom discussions this week and there is a noticeable improvement in our ELLs' oral language acquisition. Those running records that the team is using consistently are really starting to make a difference."	"Every year, more and more of our Latinx students are scoring at the proficient level on our math assessments. The gap has decreased by another 6% this year. The math department's ability to differentiate instruction has been instrumental to students' progress."
"The additional time and effort we spent preparing students for the standardized literacy test really paid off. I know that each and every one of you met with your assigned group of students regularly in order to help them practice and prepare them for the test. Our results increased by 5% from last year."	"Since we started co-constructing success criteria with students, I have noticed remarkable improvements in their ability to self-assess their work. They are also giving each other better feedback."	"There are fewer students requiring resource support this year in math. Only three needed one-on-one support this month. There were many more who required remediation in the past. You know, this speaks to the fact that the quality of classroom teaching has improved significantly."

Earl and Katz (2006) shared Beare's framework for thinking about futures and noted that the framework "can be very useful for educators" (p. 36). Beare (2001) identified three kinds of futures:

- **Possible Futures**: Futures that could happen, some of which are likely; most are unlikely to be.
- **Probable Futures:** Futures that will happen, unless something happens to throw them off course.
- **Preferable Futures:** Futures that you prefer to happen and that you will plan to make happen.

greater commitment to what *could be*. When teams realize that they can make a difference for students, it's easier to commit.

Besides the credibility of the feedback provider and causal attributions, another key aspect of efficacy-enhancing feedback relates to information provided about progress toward goals. In the examples provided (Table 5.1), note that the following goals are implied:

- Improve graduation rates.

- Increase percentage of students proficient on the standardized literacy test.

- Improve ELL oral language acquisition.

- Improve students' ability to self- and peer-assess.

- Reduce the gap between Latinx and non-Latinx students.

- Reduce the need for remediation.

The feedback provider not only attributed success to the team, but they also provided information that progress was being made toward a goal. As teams pursue goals, it's important that they understand they are making progress. During reflective practices, efficacy becomes enhanced when teams determine that they are making progress toward their goals. As teams make progress toward their goals, they can also revise them, so that they continue to strive for goals that are challenging.

> If there is no evidence yet that teams are making progress toward their goals, leaders can tap into the second most potent source of efficacy-enhancing information: vicarious experiences.
>
> Locate examples where other teams, who are faced with similar challenges and opportunities, are making progress toward their goals and share that information with team members.

Conclusion

In this chapter we explored different approaches leaders can take to support embedding reflective practices. Using structures and protocols helps facilitate evidence-based reflection. Using disaggregated data and multiple measures supports teams to continually assess their progress. Encouraging experimentation with research-based strategies and providing specific feedback about teams' work support reflection as an ongoing element of day-to-day practice.

Embedding reflective practices into educators' day-to-day work is essential. Without ongoing and frequent engagement in meaningful questions about practice, it is unlikely that teachers will shift their attributions of students' success and/or failure or increase their expectations of what students can and cannot do. These shifts are critical for teachers to build both a sense of individual and collective efficacy. As we saw with the Butte des Morts story, thoughtful structures and protocols, carefully woven into the fabric of teaching, increase educators' ability to collectively unpack previous assumptions and practices. As a result, teams are able to consider new possibilities that meet the needs of all of their students.

6 Supportive Leadership

A Leadership Mindset

On a warm day in August, Jenni arrived ready to work with the staff at a large high school. Her work that day was focused on strengthening collaboration and helping educators understand the sources of collective teacher efficacy. The principal met her at the front door and, with a friendly smile, ushered her into the building. As they were walking toward the media center, Jenni asked about the school and the principal spoke animatedly about the staff and the students. When Jenni asked the principal what messages the staff received about the day, what had been communicated, and what the teachers might be looking forward to, the principal paused and replied, "Well, I'm not really sure. *I* have no idea what to expect. The district just told me you'd be here, but it wasn't clear why."

> A leadership mindset describes the dispositions of one who
> - holds aspirational goals for themselves and their team,
> - believes in and actively cultivates leadership potential in others,
> - creates a psychologically safe environment that fosters transparency and collaboration, and
> - regularly offers and seeks feedback that leads to continuous team learning.

In our ongoing work with schools and districts, this story is often more common than readers would think. It represents a palpable disconnect between members of the leadership team, building-based leaders, and

Figure 6.1   A Model for Leading Collective Efficacy: Supportive
Leadership

educators working directly with students. When professional learning
sessions are scheduled by a few individuals choosing the next "hot topic"
from a catalog of choices, it cannot help but be a disjointed experience
for all involved.

The graphic (Figure 6.1) we have used throughout this book situates
collective teacher efficacy within the sources of efficacy and surrounded
by the enabling conditions that inform those sources. All of these are
embedded within an outer circle that indicates the critical role of leadership. Supportive leadership represents the container—the space—for
the other elements to flourish. As noted earlier, by the term *leader*, we
are referring to those in both formal and informal leadership roles.
Whether readers are system or school administrators, instructional
coaches, department chairs, division leaders, and/or classroom teachers, if you collaborate with others in a school faculty or on a team for
the purpose of improving student outcomes, you can employ the ideas
shared throughout this book.

A position of
authority does
not necessarily
demand an
authoritarian
approach to
leadership.

Having said that, however, we also recognize that without the support of formal leaders (those in positions of authority), the efforts of informal leaders will be limited at best, completely undermined at worst. But a position of authority does not necessarily demand an authoritarian approach to leadership. We are sometimes approached by vice principals, instructional coaches, and classroom teachers who express concerns about their principals' authoritarian approach to leadership. Now, we know that for some of the educators we talk to, their perceptions about their principals might be misconstrued. But when pushed for evidence, many provide compelling and disheartening examples of how their efforts in advancing this work have been stunted by their administrators. Research confirms that there are much lower levels of collective efficacy in schools characterized by authoritarian leadership.

The continuum of negotiation is actually more complicated than it might initially seem, ranging from an authoritative decision from one side, to true collaboration between all team members, and back again to an authoritative decision from the other side. This is beautifully illustrated by Patrick Dolan's (2014) 7-point decision-making continuum that defines each possible form of input (Figure 6.2). Dolan argues that prior to making critical organizational decisions, it is worthwhile to analyze the situation and decide what level of collaboration will be most effective for the process.

When considering the variety of challenges facing schools and districts, there are clearly some decisions that can safely be left to individual team members based on their expertise and/or authority. For example, teachers clearly do not need to consult with school leaders on every single instructional move they make in the classroom. School leaders clearly

> Research confirms that there are much lower levels of collective efficacy in schools characterized by authoritarian leadership.

Figure 6.2   Dolan 7-Point Decision-Making Continuum

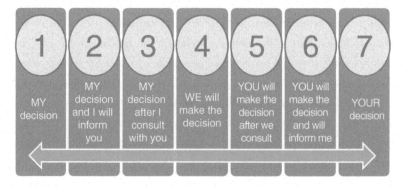

do not need to consult with teachers on every single decision they make regarding the management of the school. To attempt collaboration on every single decision would result in paralysis.

When it comes to complex systemic decisions, however, some level of collaboration typically leads to a more effective outcome. Dolan argues that a recognition of the type of collaboration prior to working toward goal consensus is highly beneficial to the process. The continuum doesn't drive the level of collaboration, but it provides insight into the type of negotiation process demanded by the situation. "If any side is uncomfortable with what you think you're agreeing to, you have to have some simple language to say, 'Where are we?' Are we doing this together? Is this ours or are you just asking my input?" (Dolan, 2014). The continuum language offers the opportunity to talk about the optimal level of collaboration.

In their study of the role of school leadership's contribution to collective teacher efficacy, Goddard et al. (2017) noted, "In schools with relatively high levels of collective efficacy, we heard frequent stories of teachers being empowered to collaborate to improve instruction, often by observing one another teaching" (p. 11). In contrast, teachers in schools with relatively low collective efficacy explained "that if they did something that ultimately worked without their principals' prior approval, they would face negative consequences, so they avoided offering ideas or solving problems on their own" (p. 12). In addition, researchers Adams and Forsyth (2006) found that enabling school structures independently accounted for the most variability in perceptions of collective teacher efficacy. They differentiated enabling school structures (procedures that lead to problem-solving among members) from hindering school structures (procedures that force conformity to rigid rules and regulations) and found a significant relationship between enabling structures and collective teacher efficacy. In other words, when hierarchy is flattened, it helps in fostering a sense of collective efficacy. When formal leaders rely solely on authoritarian leadership, it places collective teacher efficacy at risk.

DeWitt (2017) identified collaborative leadership as a more inclusive type of leadership, where fostering interdependent learning, involving all stakeholders, and co-constructing objectives are at the core of leadership practices. DeWitt noted that collaborative leaders are leaders who "collaborate more effectively around the influences that matter most and provide impact for student learning" (p. xv). DeWitt also suggested

> Goddard, et al. (2017) found that in schools characterized by low levels of collective efficacy, there was evidence of "more autocratic leadership and limited evidence of productive collaboration" (p. 12).

that the development of collective efficacy is an area of focus where collaborative leaders' efforts are best served. DeWitt said that "leaders need to think less about winning an argument and more about finding opportunities for win-win" (p. 50).

We agree that collaborative leadership is a better approach to fostering collective teacher efficacy, while we also acknowledge the significant debate over which style of leadership has the greatest impact on student outcomes. There are many adjectives that are used to describe leadership; we use supportive leadership in our model for leading collective efficacy. We might debate over terminology, but what is most important is for leaders to consider the leadership mindset and specific practices that will be the most impactful.

Marzano, Waters, and McNulty (2005) conducted a meta-analysis to determine what could be learned based on the past 35 years of research about school leadership and identified how specific responsibilities correlated with student achievement. Among the leadership responsibilities with the largest correlations to improved student outcomes, the researchers found the following: situational awareness, monitoring/evaluating, input, intellectual stimulation, and flexibility. By situational awareness, Marzano et al. mean leaders who are "aware of the details and the undercurrents regarding the functioning of the school and use this information to address current and potential problems" (p. 60). Monitoring/evaluating refers to the "extent to which the leader monitors the effectiveness of school practices in terms of their impact on student achievement" (Marzano et al., p. 55). In terms of input, the researchers refer to "the extent to which the school leader involves teachers in the design and implementation of important decisions and policies" (p. 51). Intellectual stimulation, according to the meta-analysis, refers to the leader ensuring that the "staff are aware of the most current theories and practices and makes discussion of these a regular aspect of the school's culture" (p. 42). And by flexibility, the researchers mean adaptation of leadership style to "the needs of the current situation and is comfortable with dissent" (p. 42). This was confirming for us because these specific leadership responsibilities resonate with the ideas advanced in this book.

Marzano et al. (2005) also identified "ideas/beliefs" as a leadership responsibility that is highly correlated with student achievement. They outline the following specific behaviors and characteristics associated with this responsibility as

- "possessing well-defined beliefs about schools, teaching, and learning;

- sharing beliefs about school, teaching, and learning with the staff;

- demonstrating behaviors that are consistent with beliefs" (p. 51).

To illustrate, the principal exhibits the responsibility of "ideas/beliefs" when she begins the school year by ensuring that all staff members are aware of her belief that schools "must pay particular attention to students who come from educationally disadvantaged backgrounds" (p. 51). We would argue that operating from a set of strong ideals and beliefs is at the core of effective leadership practices.

> We would argue that operating from a set of strong ideals and beliefs is at the core of effective leadership practices.

Fostering collective efficacy requires that formal school leaders focus on their own beliefs and practices. Subsequently, they can attend deeply to creating a culture of learning for all members of the educational community. How a school leader acts to shape school culture shapes the resulting climate.

How Do Leaders Shape the Conditions for All to Learn?

Before leaders can attend to building a culture of learning, they must first consider their own particular contexts. As noted earlier, situational awareness involves knowing what is happening. Leaders must distance ego from daily events and honestly appraise what is happening in the school. A careful analysis of their environment is necessary for discovering the leverage points that will allow leaders to build the desired learning culture—a culture that is collectively efficacious about their ability to meet the needs of *all* students. That analysis requires connecting deeply to the current state of affairs in a school. It requires a willingness to be honest about how the school is actually operating and how the staff is actually feeling. Leaders must be able to, as Senge et al. (2012) put it, "clearly define current reality," because so much in education is "hidden from view" (p. 8).

> Leaders must distance ego from daily events and honestly appraise what is happening in the school.

Too often leaders practice a type of "disconnected influence" in which they casually attend to the running of a school, thereby unintentionally creating a culture that cannot meet the goals of a true learning environment. Often, this comes from a lack of connection to the reality of the school climate. As Goulston and Ullmen (2013) put it, "When you practice disconnected influence, you're stuck in what we call *your here*. You can see *your* position, *your* facts, and *your* intentions clearly. But to connect with the people you're trying to influence, you need to communicate from a perspective we call *their there*. You need to see *their* position, *their* facts, and *their* intentions clearly" (p. 240). Leaders must use an honest assessment of the climate to gain situational awareness and understand the actual culture that has been established. Only then can they take strides to create the culture that will result in an ideal climate, one that fosters collective efficacy (Figure 6.3).

Figure 6.3   The Culture–Climate Relationship

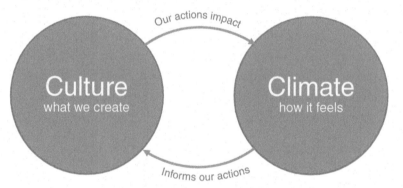

Scharmer's change management model, UTheory, describes the process of moving toward true impactful change. In UTheory, new knowledge, new thinking, and new systems can only happen when leaders truly listen so they can understand the current reality. In the book *Leading From the Emerging Future* (2013), Scharmer and Kaeufer describe this as "letting go to letting come" (Figure 6.4). In this model for change, leaders must be willing to travel down the left side of the "U" to deconstruct long-held beliefs in order to move through the bottom and rise up the right side of the "U" to welcome what might emerge. We suggest this is an essential prerequisite for school leaders intent on cultivating collective efficacy. They must let go of the preconceptions and assumptions that might prevent them from understanding the reality of their current school climate.

Figure 6.4   UTheory

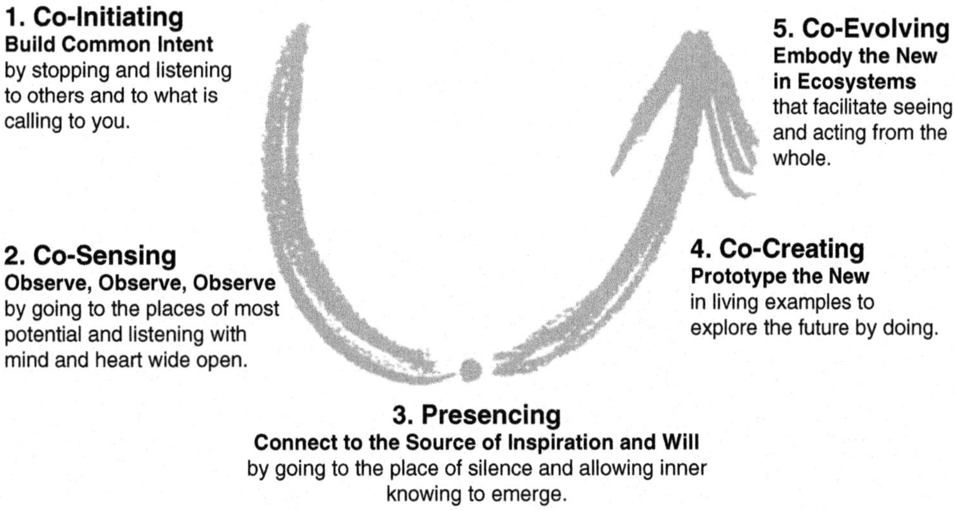

1. Co-Initiating
Build Common Intent
by stopping and listening
to others and to what is
calling to you.

5. Co-Evolving
Embody the New
in Ecosystems
that facilitate seeing
and acting from the
whole.

2. Co-Sensing
Observe, Observe, Observe
by going to the places of most
potential and listening with
mind and heart wide open.

4. Co-Creating
Prototype the New
in living examples to
explore the future by doing.

3. Presencing
Connect to the Source of Inspiration and Will
by going to the place of silence and allowing inner
knowing to emerge.

Source: Presencing Institute (n.d.). Presencing.com.

What Is the Process of "Letting Go"?

Many leaders assume organizing and building roles without first focus-ing on learning. When leaders assume the role of an *anthropologist* (see sidebar on the next page), organizations benefit from their deepened understanding of how people interact both physically and emotionally —with each other and with the institution.

VIGNETTE 6.1

Leading for Deep Reflection

It was a rainy day in Houston and the teachers at Blackberry Road Elementary had completed a full day of Opening Classroom Doors. The group was tired but still animated and discussing the many things they had noticed in their colleagues' classrooms. Looking intently at the data, they expressed concerns about missed opportunities and how they might shift their instruction.

The group ended the day with a closing check-out activity, where each teacher shared a personal insight and action step based on their experiences throughout the day. One after another, teachers shared "aha!" moments, affirmations, new ideas, and personal reflections about their own practice. When we came to the last teacher, there was a long pause and we could see her visibly preparing herself to share. "I'm new to the campus this year," she started, eyes glued to her notebook. "When I found out that I would be teaching at this school, I came in thinking that I would really have to change my teaching because of the kids that go here." She paused again, and when she looked up at the group, her eyes were full of tears. "I've been doing my students a disservice. I've been making the work easy because I figured that was all they could do. I realize now that I need to challenge them. It's my job to help them do harder work. I can't really believe that I thought that way."

In *The Ten Faces of Innovation*, Kelley (2005)—general manager of IDEO—defines 10 roles necessary for innovation to thrive in organizations. These 10 roles fall into three categories: Learning Personas, Organizing Personas, and Building Personas. The first persona in Kelley's learning category is the *Anthropologist*. Those assuming this role are willing to set aside what they think they know, observe and empathize instead of judge, and make a significant effort to experience their own environment as something they have never before encountered. To quote Marcel Proust (1929), "The only true voyage of discovery . . . would be not to visit strange lands but to possess other eyes, to behold the universe through the eyes of another, of a hundred others, to behold the hundred universes that each of them beholds" (p. 160).

Her statement was greeted by silence, her words hung in the air. It felt like a very long wait, and finally one of the instructional coaches spoke up. "I don't think you're the only one who held that belief. I bet there are more teachers here who think that way. So isn't it up to us to figure out how to change our thinking as a team? Isn't it our job to change what we expect and how we teach our students? What you said makes me think differently about my job."

Like a dam breaking, teachers began to speak up again, and this time their comments were not about what they would do as individuals but what they might do as a staff. The school and district leadership team listened, frantically taking notes, and allowed the teachers to continue sharing their ideas, well past the time when the meeting should have concluded. When the teachers finally left to help with student dismissal, the school principal and district personnel remained for a debrief session. The principal looked up and said, "Before today, I would have told you we were totally united as a staff. I think we're doing better and we see our kids' test scores going up. But after this conversation, I realize there's so much more we need to address. There's a lot more we can do because we haven't really been working as a unified team."

It can be incredibly challenging to take one's familiar environment—sometimes an organization we have worked in for years—and look at it with a new perspective. It is particularly difficult when demographics shift and educators are more and more likely to work with students from other races, ethnicities, backgrounds, and socioeconomic groups. School demographics have clearly shifted—teachers remain predominantly white and female, while the student population has become more diverse (NCES, 2018). This disparity raises important questions about how we confront inequity.

Using the lens of the Anthropologist, however, is a key first step in the journey of "letting go." How does one go about making the familiar strange? Harnessing the principles of design thinking can provide some starting points for school leaders. One of the first principles is to think about observing in a new way. Many leaders consider the term *observation* as linked to teacher evaluation. When assuming the Anthropologist role, however, observers do not gather information with an evaluatory lens; rather, they look to see what *is* by looking for things that people care about, looking at body language, looking for patterns, looking at what prompts behaviors, looking for how people make adaptations, and keeping an eye out for the unexpected.

One method of looking objectively at the current culture is to carefully consider educators' receptiveness to change (Figure 6.5). At the early stages of any implementation, collective efficacy beliefs might be high (upper-left quadrant) or might be low (lower-left quadrant). Prior to beginning the work, leaders should consider where staff beliefs lie—and act accordingly. Assuming staff members will be inquisitive and

Figure 6.5   Receptiveness to Change During Stages of Implementation Matrix

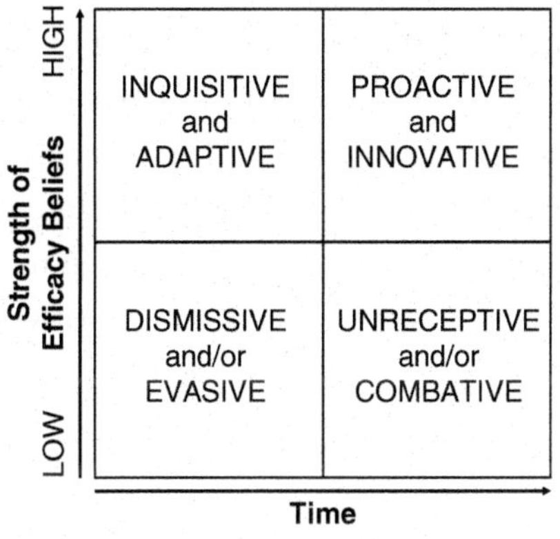

adaptive when they might actually be dismissive or invasive could result in a misstep when trying to build a culture of collective efficacy.

Diane Laughton (pseudonym), the principal of a large middle school, set out to learn more about the realities of her staff's beliefs. She began the school year by seeking opportunities to observe teacher group behaviors and logged her observations in a journal. After only a few weeks, she was able to highlight significant patterns: teachers were clearly inattentive during large group faculty meetings after about 20 minutes. They were using group planning times to grade papers and accomplish administrative tasks (rather than discussing student work or instructional strategies). In addition, Diane overheard conversations where teachers were complaining about "administrivia" and the irrelevance of many agenda items during group sessions. "I realized that meetings did not equate with accomplishment, and the faculty viewed our meetings as unnecessary interruptions in their busy days. I guess I had always assumed the scheduled meetings were a 'necessary evil' in schools. After noticing the patterns of behavior, I gave that some hard consideration. Is every agenda item actually necessary?"

Diane convened a meeting of the full staff to discuss the problem. "The irony of calling a meeting to discuss meetings was not lost on me!" she wryly recalled. Except this time, Diane changed her usual approach: instead of sharing information, she presented the problem that she had identified and asked the staff to brainstorm some solutions in small teams and then share their ideas. "It took a while to get the groups going, but by the end of the session, we had a number of interesting ideas on the table." Among those was an "information via email only" suggestion to limit the convening of physical meetings simply to share information that could easily be read via email. Diane agreed that the school leadership team would create a single email limited to a "what we all need to know today" summary to be sent to all staff at the same time each morning—and the staff agreed that they would prioritize reading that email to start their day. "It was amazing how we could keep everyone on the same page when we became intentional about how we shared information. And it was shocking to think about how often we convened meetings to discuss things that we could easily put in an email."

Once the new norm had been established, times designated for faculty meetings could be used for other purposes. "We began to design faculty meetings to be learning opportunities. Teams of teachers were responsible for designing and delivering the content. The meetings are now better attended and there is a noticeably higher level of engagement."

Another design thinking approach is to build empathy by "walking a mile in another's shoes." In 2004, Alexis Wiggins went back to high school. At the suggestion of her principal and as part of her new responsibilities as an instructional coach, she spent two days shadowing two different students (Wiggins, 2014).

It was an eye-opening experience for the 15-year teaching veteran who described it as a "mistake" that she had waited so long in her teaching career to engage in the experience. Her father, noted educator Grant Wiggins, shared Alexis's reflection on his blog and the post went viral in a matter of months. Alexis remarked later that her ability to coach teacher colleagues was far stronger based on the key takeaways from her experience. She suggests that time and distance seem to have clouded teachers' awareness of their current students' experience. Alexis noted the level of exhaustion from sitting for long stretches at a time, how mind-numbing it is to be passively receiving information in large doses, and how much of the day students are simply being controlled as they are asked to sit still and be quiet rather than engage in meaningful learning opportunities.

The experience resulted in Alexis completely rethinking how to coach teachers, reminding them of ways to incorporate movement, collaborating on varied instructional designs, and supporting a culture of positivity rather than punishment. She credits the shadowing experience as critical to her ability to unpack her previous assumptions and misconceptions. "It was so eye-opening that I wish I could go back to every class of students I ever had right now and change a minimum of 10 things."

How can leaders become anthropologists to build situational awareness? Make a point of interrupting administrative duties to create an opportunity to see "school" through a student's eyes. Cover classes for teachers to stay in tune and in touch with the realities of day-to-day

> Shane Safir (2017) wrote, "Here's the good news: If biases have been learned, they can surely be unlearned. As a leader, you can engineer experiences that build bridges and challenge misconceptions" (p. 66).

work in the classroom. These opportunities foster a leadership mindset, a willingness to dispel long-held assumptions, misconceptions, and excuses. When true understanding is in place, leaders can begin the process of "letting go to letting come."

Creating Opportunities for Informal Leadership

Readers will probably notice a common thread among the stories presented in this book: supportive leadership played an essential role in each of these. In the Maine Township chapter, *goal consensus* was achieved only after a strong district leadership team embraced the challenge of rejecting "business as usual" to focus on adult learning goals as the key to student success. This created a variety of informal leadership opportunities for teachers to serve on committees and become coaches. In our chapter on *empowered teachers*, Linden Public Schools district administrators made a critical decision to create informal teacher leadership opportunities and then carefully fostered the development of those teams over the span of several years. From our story of *cohesive teacher knowledge* in San Antonio, the cohort of 20 schools was guided by a dedicated superintendent and a team of building principals to develop structures that enabled teachers to cultivate awareness and subsequently build skills that impacted student learning. As teachers participated in Opening Classroom Doors, they played an informal leadership role by collecting and analyzing data, sharing suggestions for improvement, and bringing new thinking back to their schools.

> "Successful and sustainable improvement can never be done *to or even for* teachers. It can only be achieved *by and with* them" (Hargreaves & Fullan, 2012, p. 45).

> Goddard et al. (2017) used a mixed-methods approach to study "perspectives of teachers regarding the dimensions of school context that might explain their collective efficacy beliefs and how these beliefs in turn influence teachers' work in schools" (p. 5). One of the goals in the study was to examine specifically whether teachers indicated that the leadership of their principals influenced their collective efficacy beliefs. What consistently emerged in the data, the researchers noted, was that when teachers described their mastery experiences, how they learned vicariously, or the mood (affective states), "they frequently emphasized what their principals did to contribute in these areas" (p. 11). Schools that were high in collective efficacy were "frequently attributed to the principal and accompanied by discussions of ways in which principals empowered teachers to make decisions" (p. 12).

Conclusion

Throughout this book we have argued that positional authority is not always required for educators to step into leadership roles. That being said, there is a particular need for those who are charged with managing schools and districts to seriously consider their impact as educational leaders. To effectively build collective efficacy, those who play formal leadership positions in schools must cultivate a leadership mindset—how they perceive their role matters. A leadership mindset is critical: a willingness to let go of biases and misconceptions while embracing both the complex managerial and instructional demands of schools.

7 Conclusion

The Best Time to Plant a Tree Is 200 Years Ago. The Second Best Time Is Today.

Over the past decade, in our work with schools and districts around the world, we have noticed a shift in educator questions, from "What is collective efficacy?" to "How do we build collective efficacy?" In this book, we have shared success stories of schools and districts that have intentionally built collective efficacy by focusing on the conditions that are most likely to build educators' adaptive capacity. As school communities learn and grow together, they are able to persevere through the complex challenges of education in order to positively impact adult relationships, student achievement, and issues of inequity.

The stories in this book do not provide step-by-step guidance for other educators; rather, they provide inspiration and ideas for formal and informal leaders as they consider the complexities of their unique contexts and how they might deconstruct and reconstruct the systems that are currently in need of improvement. We have offered a model (Figure 7.1) that lays out the conditions that research has shown build the efficacy that enables educators to be adaptive and responsive to student needs. The experiences of educators in the schools and districts in this book align with research conducted over decades to confirm that building collective efficacy is worthy of educators' time and resources.

Figure 7.1 A Model for Leading Collective Efficacy

As we suggested in the preface, we encourage readers to consider the following questions when delving into these powerful stories:

1. What prompted the need for change in the school or district?

2. How did the focus on a particular enabling condition allow educators to tap into the sources of efficacy?

3. How did the highlighted enabling condition enhance the other enabling conditions and amplify the impact of teachers' work?

4. What learning protocols and designs allowed educators to structure the work so that it resulted in meaningful collaborative inquiry?

5. What lessons might we learn and apply to our unique learning community?

The model for leading collective efficacy should not be used to reduce the work of building collective teacher efficacy to following a set of instructions as if from a recipe book. There is research behind each of the five enabling conditions that fosters collective efficacy in our model, and ignoring that body of empirical evidence places collective efficacy efforts at risk. Reductive notions about collective efficacy weaken the work and might result in it becoming yet another educational buzzword that conflates superficial team-building exercises with the deep and demanding evidence-based work of collaborative inquiry.

There is research behind each of the five enabling conditions that fosters collective efficacy, and ignoring that body of empirical evidence places collective efficacy efforts at risk.

We encourage educational leaders—whether they have positional authority or play informal leadership roles—to embrace the research behind collective efficacy efforts. It is the research that gives us confidence to believe that collective efficacy has the power to impact students' lives far beyond the influences of their homes and communities. Using that solid foundation, educational leaders can build on the ideas in this book to engage in meaningful conversations in their schools and districts. It is our hope that the stories we have shared are not exceptional examples of success but a sign of the enormous shift being undertaken by educators to meet the ever-increasing complexities of 21st century learning.

Afterword

What Collective Belief
Does for Communities

We began writing this book in 2019 after working on building collective efficacy with schools and districts for many years. As we were completing our writing during the early part of 2020, the world experienced a global pandemic, forcing schools to close and for everyone to physically distance. While the lockdown proved beneficial to completing our book, it was a shocking disruption in our typically busy work life, traveling from school to school, district to district, hopping on and off planes as we pursued our work with educators around the world.

The need for schools to completely shift their methods of instruction and support with little notice and almost no preparation revealed strengths and inadequacies in educational systems. It also shone an intense spotlight on the inequities that have long been present and are now made even more evident. We noticed that schools and districts that had been highly intentional in building collective efficacy were far more resilient in the face of the extreme challenges the COVID-19 crisis posed. Their networks were in place, their methods of collaboration were well established, and there was an extremely high level of trust amongst team members that allowed them to move forward with confidence in their ability to reconfigure their instruction and support to meet the needs of their students. During the COVID-19 crisis, systems that placed trust in their teachers to make important decisions, communicated clearly and consistently, and continuously shared important learnings with ongoing support fostered the exact conditions that embed reflective practices into the work—even in its new "virtual" delivery method.

Our colleagues from Maine Township affirmed that their work on fostering collective efficacy through adult learning and coaching proved invaluable during the shift to online instruction for students. Jill Geocaris

> Schools and districts that had been highly intentional in building collective efficacy were far more resilient in the face of the extreme challenges the COVID-19 crisis posed.

115

wrote to us that teachers were joining collaborative online sessions to pose questions or share ideas. They were supporting each other's expanding understanding of technology tools. They continued their coaching traditions in ways that made a significant difference for their students.

Jenni received a remarkable email from a principal in a Manitoba school where Jenni has steadily been working to support building collective efficacy: "I thought I would let you know that our team, while seriously stressed, supported each other and found a way to go forward with incredible positivity. At our last staff meeting on Friday . . . we told our teachers two things—we trust you without reservation, and 'you, just you, are enough.' The responses from them were that they were grateful for our school's culture of collective efficacy. They knew they could trust each other, and that carried them."

Another success story came from our colleagues in Linden, where they have spent the last several years investing in instructional leadership teams across the district, fostering goal consensus, developing cohesive teacher knowledge, and empowering teachers through leadership opportunities. Their lead instructional coach, Mike Pekosz, told Stef, "It's been as smooth a transition as we could've ever hoped for. Our infrastructure helped . . . having systems in place for years." During a webinar, acting superintendent Denise Cleary affirmed that the teams that had worked together in person were continuing their work online, supporting each other and sustaining their previously well-established collaboration. After sharing their story on the webinar, Cleary sent an email to her staff: "The collaboration and support I see between colleagues has been amazing and I truly believe this is because we have established a culture of collective efficacy. We are all here for every student and no longer remain in isolation trying to figure things out. [O]ur story . . . is a good one. You are all contributing to our story, our success, and supporting one another. Thank you for all you do always."

In his book *Upstream: The Quest to Solve Problems Before They Happen* (2020), Dan Heath describes our human attachment to heroes—those who rush in to save the day during a crisis. He illuminates why we are attached to that notion: it is much easier to acknowledge a hero in action when an obvious crisis is occurring. However, it is much more challenging to recognize that true heroism occurs when someone has the foresight to address issues before they become a crisis. In fact, we often assume that when a crisis doesn't occur, it must not have been a very big problem! And, as the worldwide pandemic of 2020 has proven, that's simply not the case. There were a number of upstream solutions that might have lessened the impact of COVID-19 on our educational systems; moving forward, it is critical to reflect on what has been learned and work toward preparing for the next large-scale challenge that is sure to come.

We believe that building collective efficacy is *the* upstream solution to fostering adaptive capacity and developing systemic resilience. When organizational leaders provide the support needed to intentionally foster empowerment, cohesive knowledge, and goal consensus such that it regularly embeds reflective practices, the resulting collective efficacy creates a system that is resilient and adaptable in times of incredible challenge. In fact, those robust systems learn from the challenges to emerge stronger than before.

More importantly, when educators rushed to address inequities spotlighted by the need to close schools during the COVID-19 pandemic, they proved that these are not problems that require slow and considered solutions. The fact is, in places where schools raced to provide meals to students who were experiencing food insecurity, drove buses equipped with Wi-Fi to rural areas with no Internet access, and gathered technology devices to deliver to students' homes so they could engage in remote learning, inequities were addressed with a sense of urgency. It wasn't perfect and it wasn't universal, but these actions demonstrate our collective capacity to address inequity when priorities shift and educators are encouraged to adapt and innovate.

We invite educators to intentionally build collective efficacy because we know it is the number one impact on student achievement and clearly helps to address inequities in our educational systems. We hope educators will consider that when they focus on building collective efficacy, they are creating the armor that allows their organization to withstand adversity and bounce back stronger than before.

We believe that building collective efficacy is *the* upstream solution to fostering adaptive capacity and developing systemic resilience.

These actions demonstrate our collective capacity to address inequity when priorities shift and educators are encouraged to adapt and innovate.

Appendix A

Positive Consequences of Collective Teacher Efficacy

The Relationship Between Collective Teacher Efficacy and Student Results

There is a wealth of empirical research that shows that when teachers share the belief that through their collective actions they can positively influence student outcomes, student achievement increases. Bandura (1993) was the first to generate interest in this area by demonstrating that the effect of perceived collective efficacy on student achievement was stronger than the link between socioeconomic status and student achievement. Consistent findings have been reported in a number of other studies since (Eells, 2011). Hattie (2019) recently positioned collective teacher efficacy at the top of the list of factors that influence student achievement based on his synthesis of over 1,500 meta-analyses. In both elementary schools and secondary schools there is a compelling body of research that demonstrates a significant positive relationship between collective teacher efficacy and student achievement.

Student achievement does not happen serendipitously when collective efficacy is well established in a school. Collective teacher efficacy results in greater effort and a willingness to invest the time and energy required to attain goals. "The expectations for attainment set by perceived collective efficacy influence the diligence and tenacity with which teachers approach their work" (Goddard, LoGerfo, & Hoy, 2004, p. 420). Hoy, Sweetland, and Smith (2002) noted that "strong collective efficacy leads teachers to be more persistent in their teaching efforts, set high and reasonable goals, and overcome temporary setbacks and failures" (p. 90). This productive behavior on the part of the adults in the building leads to improved student outcomes.

A number of impactful consequences associated with collective teacher efficacy and known to promote student achievement are outlined in Table A.1.

Table A.1   Collective Teacher Efficacy: Positive Outcomes

Study	Positive Outcomes Attributed to Collective Teacher Efficacy
Boberg and Bourgeois (2016)	Promote higher levels of student emotional engagement
Caprara et al. (2003) Klassen (2010) Viel-Ruma et al. (2010) Ware and Kitsantas (2007)	Express greater job satisfaction, less stress, and greater commitment to the teaching profession
Chong et al. (2010)	Hold higher expectations and academic press
Ciani, Summers, and Easter (2008)	Teachers design more mastery experiences for students Less predominant performance goal orientations
Derrington and Angelle (2013)	Greater extent of teacher leadership
Gibbs and Powell (2011)	Less use of exclusion as a sanction for problem behavior
Goddard and Goddard (2001)	Higher individual teacher efficacy
Goddard, Skrla, and Salloum (2017)	Increase in mathematics achievement and 50% reduction in the economic disadvantage experienced by Black students
Kirby and DiPaola (2011) Lyons, Thompson, and Timmons (2016) Wilcox et al. (2014)	Increased parent and community engagement Concentrated efforts to involve parents in authentic ways Better strategies to develop and maintain family relationships
Lee, Zhang, and Yin (2011)	Greater commitment to students
Muttillo (2019)	Smaller achievement gaps
Rauf, Aluwi, and Noor (2012)	More positive attitudes toward professional development
Tiplic, Brandmo, and Elstad (2015)	Beginning teachers are less likely to leave the profession
Urton, Wilbert, and Hennemann (2014)	More positive attitudes toward remedial education
Wilcox et al. (2014)	Better qualities of academic goals, expectations, and learning opportunities More quality interventions for students at risk of dropping out

Appendix B

Enabling Conditions for Collective Teacher Efficacy Scale (EC-CTES)

In Jenni's book from 2017, *Collective Efficacy: How Educators' Beliefs Impact Student Learning*, six enabling conditions for collective efficacy were outlined. Recently, Jenni, along with Tim O'Leary and John Hattie (2020), conducted a study to test the validity of the questionnaire that appeared in that earlier work. The validation included statistical techniques (exploratory and confirmatory factor analysis) to determine composite reliability of the enabling conditions. Based on this analysis (from both a technical and theoretical perspective), the original questionnaire was revised and the Enabling Conditions for Collective Teacher Efficacy Scale (EC-CTES) was developed. It includes the following five subscales: Goal Consensus, Empowered Teachers, Cohesive Teacher Knowledge, Embedded Reflective Practices, and Supportive Leadership.

Collective efficacy scales like Goddard, Hoy, and Woolfolk Hoy's (2000) and Tschannen-Moran and Barr's (2004) are designed to capture the degree to which collective efficacy is present in a school and therefore measure teachers' future-oriented perceptions about their collective ability to motivate students, deal with disciplinary issues, and facilitate student learning. The EC-CTES measures the *antecedents* of collective efficacy. The questionnaire can be administered in schools to determine the degree to which teachers perceive the enabling conditions are in place. With this information, leaders can determine areas of strength and areas to focus their efforts in shaping environments in which teachers share the belief that individually and collectively they have the ability to impact positive change. Normative data are also available so that leaders can compare where their school is compared to others who have completed the survey.

Readers can learn more about the study at:

Donohoo, J., O'Leary, T., & Hattie, J. (2020). The design and validation of the Enabling Conditions for Collective Teacher Efficacy Scale (EC-CTES). *Journal of Professional Capital and Community*, *5*(2), 147–166. https://doi.org/10.1108/JPCC-08-2019-0020

Readers can obtain more information (e.g., how to access the questionnaire) at:

http://teacher-efficacy.com/our_services/enabling-conditions/.

Appendix C
The Stakeholder Interview

Stakeholder interviews are intentionally designed conversations with people who have a level of vested interest in your team's initiative. Stakeholders are any community members who might be able to offer useful advice about the initiative. Their input ultimately helps focus initiative design efforts. Data gathered from stakeholder interviews provide perspectives about the concerns and aspirations of those who might be impacted by the initiative; often these insights would have been difficult or impossible to obtain without expressly asking community members to discuss their thinking.

Diversity of Stakeholders

Because stakeholders are those who will be impacted by the initiative, it is important to consider the stakeholder group as broadly as possible; the more diverse the interview pool, the more insights you will gain as you develop your initiative. When organizing stakeholder interviews, development teams should continually ask, "Who is missing?"

Carefully Crafted Interview Questions

A series of interview questions guides each conversation, and it is essential to carefully craft what will be asked. While questions may vary depending on context, they should typically fall into three categories:

1. Getting to know the stakeholder

2. Questions about the stakeholder's experiences

3. Questions about the stakeholder's hopes and aspirations

We find that open-ended questions that invite stakeholders to share stories and experiences yield more powerful data than directly asking for specific information. For example, when asking a parent about scheduling, we might pose the question, "What are the pain points when registering your child for classes?" This question reveals assumptions we hold about the process itself and might skew the response. Instead, we might ask a parent, "Please share your experience of registering your child for classes." This allows the stakeholder to share a deeper and less biased response.

Structuring the Conversations

There are different ways to structure stakeholder interviews so that they are both effective and efficient. To help stakeholders feel connected to the initiative, they can be organized into teams of three, where each person plays the role of interviewer, interviewee, and note-taker. Conversations typically last 15 to 20 minutes, with roles rotating after each. In this way, every stakeholder has a chance to hear, be heard, and collect data.

Another option is to have a team of data collectors join pairs of stakeholders who hold paired conversations (with each playing the role of interviewer and interviewee). In this arrangement, the data collector is solely responsible for taking notes during the conversation. This approach tends to yield more consistent data from the interview process.

No matter the format, a harvest template (either paper or digital) should be provided for each participant that clearly defines and provides

1. the purpose of the interviews;

2. the structure of the interviews (timing, expectations);

3. questions for the interviewer to use to guide the conversation; and

4. space for the note-taker to collect data.

Harvesting the Data Using Affinity Mapping

Once interviews are completed, development teams are left with rich and insightful data that now must be organized. Affinity mapping is a process of separating the data into workable "chunks" that allow teams to understand the scope of information. We find this work is best accomplished with an analysis team that combs through the data to remove the "chunks" of information. Sticky notes are great tools, although we have also used digital solutions such as spreadsheets or virtual white boards.

The analysis team should look for

1. statistics or other key facts,

2. personal observations or stories, and

3. important quotes.

Once these "chunks" are removed from the stakeholder interview harvest sheets, they can now be organized. Organizing and reorganizing the pieces (either paper or digital) to develop categories help reveal the patterns and themes that have emerged. This is a process that requires patience, as categories often emerge, transition, collapse, and separate as they are explored. When finally organized, categories are named and patterns identified.

Value of the Process

The stakeholder process provides important insights that serve to inform initiatives in meaningful ways. We have seen project teams completely shift their goals and intentions after gaining clarity around what community members perceived to be most important. Along with clarity, stakeholder interviews provide ideas for project development as well as identification of potential barriers that might prove to be problematic. Most importantly, stakeholder interviews provide community members with an important opportunity to make their voices heard.

Appendix D

Logic Model Template

Table D.1   The Logic Model Template

Mastery Goal:

Inputs	Activities	Small-Win Goals	Mid-Journey Goals	Long-Term Performance Goals

Appendix E
World Café for Revisiting Logic Model

The World Café Protocol provides a flexible and effective format for large group conversations and is useful in helping teams revisit logic models, specifically to determine progress, mid-journey.

Total Time: 90 minutes (5 minutes to examine the logic model, 5 minutes for the introduction to World Café, 15 minutes for each round, 3–4 minutes in between each round, and 10–15 minutes for the harvest).

The environment (modeled after a café) should include small, round tables with four to six chairs. Large chart paper and markers should be available at each table. Copies of the logic model should be available for participants.

Step 1: Setting the Purpose (5 minutes)

The facilitator sets the purpose for the World Café by letting the participants know that they are going to review the logic model and determine what revisions might be needed. Provide time for the participants to review the logic model. The questions posed during each round of conversation should be carefully crafted to encourage reflection on both the long-term vision and mid-journey goals.

Step 2: Introduction to the World Café (5 minutes)

The facilitator shares information about the World Café process, sharing the café etiquette and putting participants at ease. Participants are informed that there will be three rounds of discussion, prompted each time by a question(s). People are encouraged to consider the question, listen to others' perspectives, and share their own in relation to possible revisions to the logic model. Participants are encouraged to capture the ideas on the chart paper using words, images, and/or symbols. They are encouraged to connect ideas and use probing questions to fully under-stand each other's ideas and/or contributions. Each table group is asked to nominate (or have someone volunteer) to host the conversation. The table host will remain at the same table for all three rounds and it is their responsibility to welcome new people (for each new round) and summarize previous discussions (referring to what was captured on the chart paper).

Step 3: Round 1 (15 minutes)

The process begins with the first of three rounds of conversation for the small group seated around each table. The facilitator shares the first ques-tion and sets a timer for 15 minutes. The first question should encour-age conversation that reflects on the experiences that are relevant to the long-term goal. For example, *what are your experiences related to our long-term vision? Given our goal, what makes those experiences significant?*

With 4 to 5 minutes remaining in the round, the facilitator provides a time check for participants to begin pulling their conversations to a close by identifying the major patterns or themes that emerged. One or two themes are recorded on large-format sticky notes and then shared to make the thinking that has emerged from the first round of conver-sation visible to the entire group.

Step 4: Move to Round 2 (3–4 minutes)

At the end of 15 minutes, each member of the group moves to a new table of their choice, with the intention of creating new con-versational groups. One goal of the World Café is to diversify the group members—and subsequently, the thinking—by mixing up the conversation participants as much as possible between rounds. The host remains at the table, welcomes new participants, and briefly shares what was discussed during the first round.

Step 5: Round 2 (15 minutes)

The facilitator shares the second question and sets a timer for 15 min-utes. Participants are encouraged to record their thoughts, ideas, and suggestions on chart paper. The question for the second round should focus the conversation toward mid-journey goals. For example, *what are some of the successes and challenges emerging in our work toward mid-journey goals?* As with round 1, the facilitator provides a time check with 4 to 5 minutes remaining in the round, asking participants to notice patterns or themes that are emerging. Those are recorded on large-format sticky notes shared to make thinking visible to the entire group.

Step 6: Move to Round 3 (3–4 minutes)

At the end of round 2, each member of the group moves to a new table of their choice. Again, the host remains at the table, welcomes new participants, and briefly shares what was discussed during the second round.

Step 7: Round 3 (15 minutes)

The facilitator shares the final question and sets a timer for 15 minutes. Participants are encouraged to record their thoughts, ideas, and suggestions on the chart paper. The third question should be highly reflective and consider possible revisions to the logic model. For example, *given the successes and challenges we have experienced, what course corrections might we need as we work toward our long-term vision?* With 4 to 5 minutes remaining in the round, the facilitator should provide a time check, asking the participants to capture their most important thinking about goal revision on large-format sticky notes.

Step 8: Harvest (10–15 minutes)

In between rounds, it is helpful for the facilitator to organize the shared sticky notes to cluster similar ideas. As participants move to new tables between rounds, they are invited to stroll past the visible display so they can be aware of the patterns and themes emerging across the larger group.

After the final round, the facilitator should invite participants to share what they have noticed in the large group's thinking. What overarching patterns have emerged from all rounds of conversation? What might that imply about the need to rethink previously established goals?

Appendix F
Opening Classroom Doors Logistics

When considering how to structure Opening Classroom Doors, the visitation schedule and agenda are critical elements. Proactively addressing potential disruptions allows participants to focus on their data collection and analysis tasks.

The number of team members and visiting teams depends on the size of the school. We suggest teams be no larger than three or four visitors so as to minimize instructional disruption. Each member of the visiting team is assigned a Look-For to focus their data collection. Therefore, teams of three can address three Look-Fors while teams of four can address four Look-Fors.

Schedules for visits should be long enough to collect valuable data and not so long that visitors are limited to only a few experiences. We recommend that the observation times be structured to allow for data collection to occur during optimal instruction time for students. We also recommend teams visit classrooms in 20-minute intervals, with teams rotating so that each period of instruction is observed for a total of 40 minutes. This provides a longer observation period in terms of data collection but minimizes the time teachers spend in one classroom to reduce bias and increase objectivity. Following (Tables F.1–4) are several sample schedules that demonstrate how to accommodate different-sized schools.

Table F.1   Sample Schedule for Two Groups (Six Total Visitors) Collecting Data on Three Look-Fors in Six Classrooms

Sample Times (adjust as needed) ↓	Home Team A Look-For 1. Team Member Look-For 2. Team Member Look-For 3. Team Member	Home Team B Look-For 1. Team Member Look-For 2. Team Member Look-For 3. Team Member
9:30–9:50 a.m.	Classroom 1	Classroom 2
9:50–10:10 a.m.	Classroom 2	Classroom 1
BREAK		
10:15–10:35 a.m.	Classroom 3	Classroom 4
10:35–10:55 a.m.	Classroom 4	Classroom 3
BREAK		
11:00–11:20 a.m.	Classroom 5	Classroom 6
11:20–11:40 a.m.	Classroom 6	Classroom 5

Table F.2   Sample Schedule for Three Groups (12 Total Visitors) Collecting Data on Four Look-Fors in Nine Classrooms

Sample Times (adjust as needed) ↓	Home Team A Look-For 1. Team Member Look-For 2. Team Member Look-For 3. Team Member Look-For 4. Team Member	Home Team B Look-For 1. Team Member Look-For 2. Team Member Look-For 3. Team Member Look-For 4. Team Member	Home Team C Look-For 1. Team Member Look-For 2. Team Member Look-For 3. Team Member Look-For 4. Team Member
9:30–9:50 a.m.	Classroom 1	Classroom 2	Classroom 3
9:50–10:10 a.m.	Classroom 3	Classroom 1	Classroom 2
BREAK			
10:15–10:35 a.m.	Classroom 4	Classroom 5	Classroom 6
10:35–10:55 a.m.	Classroom 6	Classroom 4	Classroom 5
BREAK			
11:00–11:20 a.m.	Classroom 7	Classroom 8	Classroom 9
11:20–11:40 a.m.	Classroom 9	Classroom 7	Classroom 8

Table F.3   Sample Schedule for Four Groups (12 Total Visitors) Collecting Data on Four Look-Fors in 12 Classrooms

Sample Times (adjust as needed) →	Home Team A Look-For 1. Team Member Look-For 2. Team Member Look-For 3. Team Member	Home Team B Look-For 1. Team Member Look-For 2. Team Member Look-For 3. Team Member	Home Team C Look-For 1. Team Member Look-For 2. Team Member Look-For 3. Team Member	Home Team D Look-For 1. Team Member Look-For 2. Team Member Look-For 3. Team Member
9:30–9:50 a.m.	Classroom 1	Classroom 2	Classroom 7	Classroom 8
9:50–10:10 a.m.	Classroom 2	Classroom 1	Classroom 8	Classroom 7
BREAK				
10:15–10:35 a.m.	Classroom 3	Classroom 4	Classroom 9	Classroom 10
10:35–10:55 a.m.	Classroom 4	Classroom 3	Classroom 10	Classroom 9
BREAK				
11:00–11:20 a.m.	Classroom 5	Classroom 6	Classroom 11	Classroom 12
11:20–11:40 a.m.	Classroom 6	Classroom 5	Classroom 12	Classroom 11

Table F.4   Sample Schedule for Six Groups (24 Total Visitors) Collecting Data on Four Look-Fors in 18 Classrooms

Sample Times (adjust as needed) →	Home Team A — Look-For 1. Team Member / Look-For 2. Team Member / Look-For 3. Team Member / Look-For 4. Team Member	Home Team B — Look-For 1. Team Member / Look-For 2. Team Member / Look-For 3. Team Member / Look-For 4. Team Member	Home Team C — Look-For 1. Team Member / Look-For 2. Team Member / Look-For 3. Team Member / Look-For 4. Team Member	Home Team D — Look-For 1. Team Member / Look-For 2. Team Member / Look-For 3. Team Member / Look-For 4. Team Member	Home Team E — Look-For 1. Team Member / Look-For 2. Team Member / Look-For 3. Team Member / Look-For 4. Team Member	Home Team F — Look-For 1. Team Member / Look-For 2. Team Member / Look-For 3. Team Member / Look-For 4. Team Member
9:30–9:50 a.m.	Class 1	Class 2	Class 7	Class 8	Class 13	Class 14
9:50–10:10 a.m.	Class 2	Class 1	Class 8	Class 7	Class 14	Class 13
BREAK						
10:15–10:35 a.m.	Class 3	Class 4	Class 9	Class 10	Class 15	Class 16
10:35–10:55 a.m.	Class 4	Class 3	Class 10	Class 9	Class 16	Class 15
BREAK						
11:00–11:20 a.m.	Class 5	Class 6	Class 11	Class 12	Class 17	Class 18
11:20–11:40 a.m.	Class 6	Class 5	Class 12	Class 11	Class 18	Class 17

The agenda for a day of Opening Classroom Doors is created and shared with all educators. Table F.5 is a sample agenda (schools adjust times to accommodate their schedule as needed).

Table F.5   Sample Agenda

WELCOME!	
7:45–8:00 a.m.	Teams arrive/Complete thank-you notes to leave behind in classroom
PREPARATION	
8:00–8:05 a.m.	**Welcome:** Participants learn the expectations for the day
8:05–8:15 a.m.	**Setting the Stage:** Participants are introduced to background information about the school and review the Point of Inquiry (POI) and Look-Fors
8:15–8:20 a.m.	**Classroom Visit Guidelines**
8:20–8:30 a.m.	**HOME TEAM Logistical Planning:** Participants assign roles (timekeeper, thank-yous, navigator)
8:30–8:55 a.m.	**LOOK-FORS TEAM Clarifying Data Collection:** Participants move to Look-Fors groups to create a coherent approach to collecting data around the particular Look-For they are assigned
9:00–11:10 a.m.	**CLASSROOM VISITS (See schedule)**
11:10–11:40 a.m.	**LUNCH**
ANALYSIS	
11:50 a.m. –12:40 p.m.	**LOOK-FORS TEAM:** Mesh data with your Look-Fors team by determining unit of measure and data to be displayed
12:40–12:50 p.m.	**HOME TEAM:** Share initial data findings with Home Team to connect with the big picture (POI)
12:50–1:00 p.m.	**BREAK**
1:00–2:00 p.m.	**LOOK-FORS TEAM** • Designate a timekeeper/consensus builder • Develop data charts for host school
2:00–2:20 p.m.	**LOOK-FORS TEAM Sharing**
2:20–2:50 p.m.	**HOME TEAM Data Analysis:** Teams consider a focused data point, why it's important, and a logical best next step
2:50–3:00 p.m.	**Personal Reflection**

References

Adams, C., & Forsyth, P. (2006). Proximate sources of collective teacher efficacy. *Journal of Educational Administration, 44*(6), 625–642.

Bandura, A. (1977). Self-efficacy: Toward a unifying theory of behavioral change. *Psychological Review, 84*(2), 191–215.

Bandura, A. (1986). *Social foundations of thought and action: A social cognitive theory.* Englewood Cliffs, NJ: Prentice Hall.

Bandura, A. (1993). Perceived self-efficacy in cognitive development and functioning. *Educational Psychologist, 28*(2), 117–148.

Bandura, A. (1997). *Self-efficacy: The exercise of control.* New York, NY: W.H. Freeman and Company.

Bandura, A. (1998). Personal and collective efficacy in human adaptation and change. In J. G. Adair, D. Belanger, & K. L. Dion (Eds.), *Advances in psychological science: Vol. 1, Personal, social, and cultural aspects* (pp. 51–71). Hove, UK: Psychology Press.

Bandura, A. (2000). Exercise of human agency through collective efficacy. *Current Directions in Psychological Science, 9*(3), 75–78.

Beare, H. (2001). *Creating the future school.* London: Routledge Falmer.

Bernhardt, V. L. (1998, March). Invited Monograph No. 4. California Association for Supervision and Curriculum Development (CASCD).

Birk, C., & Larson, G. (2019). *PLC 2.0: Collaborating for observable impact in today's schools.* Oshkosh, WI: FIRST Educational Resources.

Boberg, J., & Bourgeois, S. (2016). The effects of integrated transformational leadership on achievement. *Journal of Educational Administration, 54*(3), 357–374.

Bruce, C., & Flynn, T. (2013). Assessing the effects of collaborative professional learning: Efficacy shifts in a three-year mathematics study. *Alberta Journal of Educational Research*, *58*(4), 691–709.

Budge, K. M., & Parrett, W. (2018). *Disrupting poverty: Five powerful classroom practices*. Alexandria, VA: ASCD.

Caprara, G., Barbaranelli, C., Borgogni, L., Petitta, L., & Rubinacci, A. (2003). Teachers', school staff's and parents' efficacy beliefs as determinants of attitudes toward school. *European Journal of Psychology of Education*, *18*(1), 15–31.

Chong, W., Klassen, R., Huan, V., Wong, I., & Kates, A. (2010). The relationships among school types, teacher efficacy beliefs, and academic climate: Perspective from Asian middle schools. *The Journal of Educational Research*, *103*(3), 183–190.

Ciani, K., Summers, J., & Easter, M. (2008). A top-down analysis of high school teacher motivation. *Contemporary Educational Psychology*, *33*, 533–560.

City, E. (2011). Learning from instructional rounds. *Educational Leadership*, *69*(2), 36–41.

City, E., Elmore, E., Fiarman, S., & Teitel, L. (2009). *Instructional rounds in education: A network approach to improving teaching and learning*. Cambridge, MA: Harvard Education Press.

Consensus. (n.d.). In *Cambridge Dictionary*. New York, NY: Cambridge University Press. Retrieved from https://dictionary.cambridge.org/us/dictionary/english/consensus

Corwin Visible Learning Plus. (2019). Global research database. Retrieved March 17, 2020, from http://www.visiblelearningmetax.com/Influences and https://www.visiblelearning.com/content/faq#Homework

Csikszentmihalyi, M. (1990). *Flow: The psychology of optimal experience*. New York, NY: HarperPerennial.

Day, C., Kington, A., Stobart, G., & Sammons, P. (2006). The personal and professional selves of teachers: Stable and unstable identities. *British Educational Research Journal*, *32*(4), 601–616.

Delpit, L. (2006). *Other people's children: Cultural conflict in the classroom*. New York, NY: New Press.

Derrington, M., & Angelle, P. (2013). Teacher leadership and collective efficacy: Connections and links. *International Journal of Teacher Leadership*, *4*(1), 1–13.

DeWitt, P. (2017). *Collaborative leadership: Six influences that matter most.* Thousand Oaks, CA: Corwin.

DeWitt, P. (2020). *Instructional leadership: Creating practice out of theory.* Thousand Oaks, CA: Corwin.

Dolan, P. W. (2014, March). Presentation at CalTURN, the California Teacher Union Reform Network in Sacramento.

Donohoo, J. (2017). *Collective efficacy: How educators' beliefs impact student learning.* Thousand Oaks, CA: Corwin.

Donohoo, J., Hattie, J., & Eells, R. (2018). The power of collective efficacy. *Educational Leadership, 75*(6), 41–44.

Donohoo, J., & Katz, S. (2020). *Quality implementation: Leveraging collective efficacy to make "what works" actually work.* Thousand Oaks, CA: Corwin.

Donohoo, J., O'Leary, T., & Hattie, J. (2020). The design and validation of the Enabling Conditions for Collective Teacher Efficacy Scale (EC-CTES). *Journal of Professional Capital and Community, 5*(2). https://doi.org/10.1108/JPCC-08-2019-0020

Earl, L., & Katz, S. (2006). *Leading schools in a data-rich world: Harnessing data for school improvement.* Thousand Oaks, CA: Corwin.

Easton, L. B. (2009). *Protocols for professional learning.* Alexandria, VA: Association for Supervision and Curriculum Development.

Education Trust. (2019, December 9). 5 things to advance equity in access to and success in advanced coursework. Retrieved from Education Trust website April 18, 2020. https://edtrust.org/resource/5-things-to-advance-equity-in-access-to-and-success-in-advanced-coursework/

Eells, R. (2011). *Meta-analysis of the relationship between collective efficacy and student achievement* (Unpublished doctoral dissertation). Loyola University of Chicago.

Evans, A. (2009). No Child Left Behind and the quest for educational equity: The role of teachers' collective sense of efficacy. *Leadership and Policy in Schools, 8*, 64–91.

Feagin, J. R., & Barnett, B. M. (2004, August 31). Success and failure: How systemic racism trumped the *Brown v. Board of Education* decision. *Illinois Law Review.* Accessed May 6, 2020, from https://illinoislawreview.org/print/volume-2004-issue-5/success-and-failure-how-systemic-racism-trumped-the-brown-v-board-of-education-decision/

Gibbs, S., & Powell, B. (2011). Teacher efficacy and pupil behaviour: The structure of teachers' individual and collective beliefs and their relationship with numbers of pupils excluded from school. *British Journal of Educational Psychology, 82*(4), 564–584.

Goddard, R. D. (2002). Collective efficacy and school organization: A multilevel analysis influence in schools. *Theory and Research in Educational Administration, 1*, 169–184.

Goddard, R. D., & Goddard, Y. (2001). A multilevel analysis of the relationship between teacher and collective efficacy in urban schools. *Teaching and Teacher Education, 17*(7), 807–818.

Goddard, R. D., Hoy, W. K., & Woolfolk Hoy, A. (2000). Collective teacher efficacy: Its meaning, measure, and impact on student achievement. *American Educational Research Journal, 37*(2), 479–507.

Goddard, R., Goddard, Y., Kim, E., & Miller, R. (2015). A theoretical and empirical analysis of the roles of instructional leadership, teacher collaboration, and collective efficacy beliefs in support of student learning. *American Journal of Education, 121*, 501–530.

Goddard, R., LoGerfo, L., & Hoy, W. (2004). High school accountability: The role of perceived collective efficacy. *Educational Policy, 18*(3), 403–425.

Goddard, R., Skrla, L., & Salloum, S. (2017). The role of collective efficacy in closing student achievement gaps: A mixed methods study of school leadership for excellence and equity. *Journal of Education for Students Placed at Risk, 22*(4), 220–236.

Goulston, M. Y., & Ullmen, J. (2013). *Real influence: Persuade without pushing and gain without giving in.* New York, NY: Amacom.

Gully, S., Incalcaterra, K., Joshi, A., & Beaubein, J. M. (2002). A meta-analysis of team-efficacy, potency, and performance: Interdependence and level of analysis as moderators of observed relationships. *Journal of Applied Psychology, 87*(5), 819–832.

Haberman, M. (1991). The pedagogy of poverty versus good teaching. *Phi Delta Kappan, 73*, 290–294.

Hall, K. (2019). *Stories that stick: How storytelling can captivate customers, influence audiences, and transform your business.* New York, NY: HarperCollins.

Hammond, Z. (2015). *Culturally responsive teaching and the brain: Promoting authentic engagement and rigor among culturally and linguistically diverse students.* Thousand Oaks, CA: Corwin.

Hargreaves, A., & Fullan, M. (2012). *Professional capital: Transforming teaching in every school.* New York, NY: Teachers College Press.

Hattie, J. (2009). *Visible Learning: A synthesis of over 800 meta-analyses relating to achievement.* New York, NY: Routledge.

Hattie, J. (2019). Visible Learning. http://www.visiblelearningmetax.com/influences/view/collective_teacher_efficacy

Heath, D. (2020). *Upstream: The quest to solve problems before they happen.* New York: Avid Reader Press.

Hidi, H., & Harackiewicz, J. (2000). Motivating the academically unmotivated: A critical issue for the 21st century. *Review of Educational Research, 70*(2), 151–179.

Hord, S., Rutherford, W. L., Huling-Austin, L., & Hall, G. E. (2014). *Taking charge of change.* Austin, TX: SEDL.

Hoy, W., Sweetland, S., & Smith, P. (2002). Toward an organizational model of achievement in high schools: The significance of collective efficacy. *Educational Administration Quarterly, 38*(1), 77–93.

Hoy, W. K., Smith, P. A., & Sweetland, S. R. (2003). A test of a model of school achievement in rural schools: The significance of collective efficacy. In W. K. Hoy & C. G. Miskel (Eds.), *Theory and research in educational administration* (pp. 185–202). Greenwich, CT: Information Age.

Ingersoll, R., Dougherty, P., & Sirinides, P. (2017). *School leadership counts.* Philadelphia: University of Pennsylvania Graduate School of Education.

Jensen, E. (2009). *Teaching with poverty in mind: What being poor does to kids' brains and what schools can do about it.* Alexandria, VA: ASCD.

Johnson, J. (2019, November 19). School report cards show under 50% of District 207 students proficient in math, language arts, science. *Chicago Tribune.* Accessed May 6, 2020, from https://www.chicagotribune.com/suburbs/park-ridge/ct-prh-d207-report-cards-tl-1121-20191119-ikrporbcgfcwvgqxbolmjiydfm-story.html

Katz, S., & Dack, L. (2013). *Intentional interruption: Breaking down learning barriers to transform professional practice.* Thousand Oaks, CA: Corwin.

Katz, S., Earl, L., & Ben Jaafar, S. (2009). *Building and connecting learning communities: The power of networks for school improvement.* Thousand Oaks, CA: Corwin.

Kelley, T., with Littman, J. (2005). *The ten faces of innovation: IDEO's strategies for beating the devil's advocate and driving creativity throughout your organization.* New York, NY: Doubleday.

Killion, J. (2008). *Assessing impact: Evaluating staff development.* Thousand Oaks, CA: Corwin.

Killion, J. (2018). *Assessing impact: Evaluating professional learning* (3rd ed.). Thousand Oaks, CA: Corwin.

Klassen, R. (2010). Teacher stress: The mediating role of collective efficacy beliefs. *The Journal of Educational Research, 103*(5), 342–350.

Kirby, M., & DiPaola, M. (2011). Academic optimism and community engagement in urban schools. *Journal of Educational Administration, 49*(5), 542–562.

Kurz, T. B., & Knight, S. (2003). An exploration of the relationship among teacher efficacy, collective teacher efficacy, and goal consensus. *Learning Environments Research, 7*(2), 111–128.

Latham, G., & Seijts, G. (1999). The effects of proximal and distal goals on performance on a moderately complex task. *Journal of Organizational Behavior, 20*(4), 421–429.

Lee, J., Zhang, Z., & Yin, H. (2011). A multilevel analysis of the impact of a professional learning community, faculty trust in colleagues and collective efficacy on teacher commitment to students. *Teaching and Teacher Education, 27*(5), 820–830.

Lindsley, D., Brass, D., & Thomas, J. (1995). Efficacy-performance spirals: A multilevel perspective. *Academy of Management Review, 20*(3), 645–678.

Livingston, C. (1992). Introduction: Teacher leadership for restructured schools. In C. Livingston (Ed.), *Teachers as leaders: Evolving roles.* NEA School Restructuring Series. Washington, DC: National Education Association.

Lyons, W., Thompson, A., & Timmons, V. (2016). We are inclusive. We are a team. Let's just do it: Commitment, collective efficacy, and agency in four inclusive schools. *International Journal of Inclusive Education, 20*(8), 889–907.

Maine Township District 207. (2020, March 4). Adult learning. Maine Township district website. https://maine207.org/building-the-learner/#alignments

Marzano, R. E. (2012). Art and science of teaching/It's how you use a strategy. *Educational Leadership, 69*(4), 88–89.

Marzano, R., & Waters, T. (2009). *District leadership that works: Striking the right balance.* Bloomington, IL: Solution Tree Press.

Marzano, R., Waters, T., & McNulty, B. (2005). *School leadership that works: From research to results.* Alexandria, VA: Association for Supervision and Curriculum Development.

Mattern, K., Radunzel, J., & Harmston, M. (2016, August). ACT composite score by family income. ACT Research & Policy. Retrieved April 19, 2020, from https://www.act.org/content/dam/act/unsecured/documents/R1604-ACT-Composite-Score-by-Family-Income.pdf

Muttillo, A. J. (2019). *Schools of excellence and equity: Closing achievement gaps through collective efficacy* [Unpublished doctoral dissertation]. University of North Carolina at Chapel Hill. https://cdr.lib.unc.edu/concern/dissertations/9p290b59w

National Center for Education Statistics (NCES). (2018). Characteristics of public school teachers. Washington, DC: Author. Accessed April 22, 2020, from https://nces.ed.gov/programs/coe/indicator_clr.asp

National Center for Education Statistics (NCES). (2019). ACS-ED District Demographic Dashboard 2014–18: Linden City School District, NJ. Retrieved from https://nces.ed.gov/Programs/Edge/ACSDashboard/3408610

Noguera, P., Darling-Hammond, L., & Friedlaender, D. (2015). *Equal opportunity for deeper learning.* Students at the Center: Deeper Learning Research Series. Boston, MA: Jobs for the Future.

Pink, D. H. (2009). *Drive: The surprising truth about what motivates us.* New York, NY: Penguin Group.

Popham, J. W. (2013). *Evaluating America's teachers: Mission possible?* Thousand Oaks, CA: Corwin.

Presencing Institute. (n.d.). Theory U. https://www.presencing.org/aboutus/theory-u

Proust, M. (1929). The captive. In *Remembrance of things past.* C. K. Scott Moncrieff, trans. London: Alfred A. Knopf.

Race Matters Institute. (2014, April 2). *Racial equality or racial equity? The difference it makes.* Accessed April 21, 2020, from https://viablefuturescenter.org/racemattersinstitute/2014/04/02/racial-equality-or-racial-equity-the-difference-it-makes

Rauf, P., Aluwi, A., & Noor, N. (2012). The effect of school culture on the management of professional development in secondary schools in Malaysia. *The Malaysian Online Journal of Educational Science, 2*(3), 41–51.

Reeves, D. (2010). *Transforming professional development into student results.* Alexandria, VA: ASCD.

Riordan, M., Klein, E. J., & Gaynor, C. (2019). Teaching for equity and deeper learning: How does professional learning transfer to teachers' practice and influence students' experiences? *Equity & Excellence in Education, 52*(2–3), 327–345.

Robinson, V. (2018). *Reduce change to increase improvement.* Corwin Impact Leadership Series. Thousand Oaks, CA: Corwin.

Robinson, V., Hohepa, M., & Lloyd, C. (2009). *School leadership and student outcomes: Identifying what works and why: Best evidence synthesis iteration [BES].* Wellington, New Zealand: Ministry of Education.

Ross, J., Hogaboam-Gray, A., & Gray, P. (2004). Prior student achievement, collaborative school processes, and collective teacher efficacy. *Leadership and Policy in Schools, 3*(3), 163–188.

Rubie-Davis, C., Hattie, J., & Hamilton, R. (2006). Expecting the best for students: Teacher expectations and academic outcomes. *British Journal of Educational Psychology, 76*(Pt. 3), 429–444.

Safir, S. (2017). *The listening leader: Creating the conditions for equitable school transformation.* San Francisco, CA: Jossey-Bass.

Salanova, M., Rodriguez-Sanchez, A., Schaufeli, W., & Cifre, E. (2014). Flowing together: A longitudinal study of collective efficacy and collective flow among workgroups. *The Journal of Psychology: Interdisciplinary and Applied, 148*(4), 435–455.

Sandoval, J., Challoo, L., & Kupczynski, L. (2011). The relationship between teachers' collective efficacy and student achievement at economically disadvantaged middle school campuses. *I-managers Journal of Educational Psychology, 5*(1), 9–23.

Scharmer, O., & Kaeufer, K. (2013). *Leading from the emerging future: From ego-system to eco-system economies.* San Francisco, CA: Berrett-Kohler.

Schechter, C., & Qadach, M. (2012). Toward an organizational model of change in elementary schools: The contribution of organizational learning mechanisms. *Educational Administration Quarterly, 48*(1), 116–153.

Senge, P., Cambron-McCabe, N., Lucas, T., & Smith, B. (2012). *Schools that learn: A fifth discipline fieldbook for educators, parents, and everyone who cares about education*. New York, NY: Crown Business.

Snowden, D. (2020, January 21). *Reimagining leadership 2030* [Video file]. Retrieved from https://youtu.be/5VgU-ClYsvs

Teacher Leadership Exploratory Consortium (TLEC). (2017). *Teacher leader model standards*. Retrieved from https://www.ets.org/s/education_topics/teaching_quality/pdf/teacher_leader_model_standards.pdf

Texas Tribune. (n.d.). San Antonio ISD. Public Schools Explorer. Retrieved from https://schools.texastribune.org/districts/san-antonio-isd/

Tiplic, D., Brandmo, C., & Elstad, E. (2015). Antecedents of Norwegian beginning teachers' turnover intentions. *Cambridge Journal of Education, 45*(4), 451–474.

TNTP. (2018). *The opportunity myth: What students can show us about how school is letting them down—and how to fix it.* https://tntp.org/assets/documents/TNTP_The-Opportunity-Myth_Web.pdf

Tschannen-Moran, M., & Barr, M. (2004). Fostering student learning: The relationship of collective teacher efficacy and student achievement. *Leadership and Policy in Schools, 3*(3), 189–209.

Urton, K., Wilbert, J., & Hennemann, T. (2014). Attitudes towards inclusion and self-efficacy of principals and teachers. *Learning Disabilities: A Contemporary Journal, 12*(2), 151–168.

Viel-Ruma, K., Houchins, D., Jolivette, K., & Benson, G. (2010). Efficacy beliefs of special educators: The relationships among collective efficacy, teacher self-efficacy, and job satisfaction. *Teacher Education and Special Education, 33*(3), 225–233.

Ware, H., & Kitsantas, A. (2007). Teacher and collective efficacy beliefs as predictors of professional commitment. *The Journal of Educational Research, 100*(5), 303–310.

Wheatley, M. J. (2006). *Leadership and the new science. Discovering order in a chaotic world* (3rd ed). San Francisco, CA: Berrett-Koehler.

Wiggins, A. (2014, October). A veteran teacher turned coach shadows 2 students for 2 days—a sobering experience. Granted, and . . . Thoughts on education by Grant Wiggins blog. Retrieved March 19, 2020, from https://grantwiggins.wordpress.com/2014/10/10/a-veteran-teacher-turned-coach-shadows-2-students-for-2-days-a-sobering-lesson-learned/

Wilcox, K., Angelis, J., Baker, L., & Lawson, H. (2014). The value of people, place and possibilities: A multiple case study of rural high school completion. *Journal of Research in Rural Education, 29*(9), 1–18.

Wisconsin Department of Public Instruction. (2019). *2018–19 accountability report cards: Closing gaps guide.* https://dpi.wi.gov/sites/default/files/imce/accountability/pdf/Closing_Gaps_Guide_2018-19_Final.pdf

Zak, P. J. (2015, January–February). Why inspiring stories make us react: The neuroscience of narrative. *Cerebrum.* Retrieved May 15, 2020, from https://www.ncbi.nlm.nih.gov/pmc/articles/PMC4445577/

Index

Solutions YOU WANT | Experts YOU TRUST | Results YOU NEED

EVENTS

> > > **INSTITUTES**

Corwin Institutes provide large regional events where educators collaborate with peers and learn from industry experts. Prepare to be recharged and motivated!

corwin.com/institutes

ON-SITE PD

> > > **ON-SITE PROFESSIONAL LEARNING**

Corwin on-site PD is delivered through high-energy keynotes, practical workshops, and custom coaching services designed to support knowledge development and implementation.

corwin.com/pd

> > > **PROFESSIONAL DEVELOPMENT RESOURCE CENTER**

The PD Resource Center provides school and district PD facilitators with the tools and resources needed to deliver effective PD.

corwin.com/pdrc

ONLINE

> > > **ADVANCE**

Designed for K–12 teachers, Advance offers a range of online learning options that can qualify for graduate-level credit and apply toward license renewal.

corwin.com/advance

Contact a PD Advisor at (800) 831-6640 or visit www.corwin.com for more information

A SAGE Publishing Company

Helping educators make the greatest impact

CORWIN HAS ONE MISSION: to enhance education through intentional professional learning.

We build long-term relationships with our authors, educators, clients, and associations who partner with us to develop and continuously improve the best evidence-based practices that establish and support lifelong learning.